Blue Horizons

Blue Horizons

Dispatches from Distant Seas

Beth A. Leonard

International Marine/McGraw-Hill

Camden, Maine • New York • Chicago
San Francisco • Lisbon • London • Madrid
Mexico City • Milan • New Delhi • San Juan
Seoul • Singapore • Sydney • Toronto

The *McGraw·Hill* Companies

1 2 3 4 5 6 7 8 9   DOC DOC   0 9 8 7 6

Library of Congress Cataloging-in-Publication Data

Leonard, Beth A.
   Blue horizons : dispatches from distant seas / Beth A. Leonard.
      p. cm.
   ISBN 0-07-147958-9 (hardcover : alk. paper)
   1. Leonard, Beth A.—Travel.   2. Voyages around the world.   I. Title.
   G440.L56L457 2007
   910.4'1—dc22

                                                        2006012381

ISBN-13: 978-0-07147958-5
ISBN-10: 0-07-147958-9
Photographs by the author
Design by Dennis A. Anderson
Map on pages viii–ix by International Mapping.

DEDICATION

This book is dedicated to three people who taught me about living life fully and facing death with grace and courage.

Walker Vought (b. March 29, 1942; d. September 9, 2002): I would live my life with your unbounded enthusiasm and infectious good cheer, and approach every new project with your unflagging energy and steadfast determination.

Eric Dahn (b. September 30, 1945; d. February 28, 2005): I would face my death as bravely and defiantly as you did, with your unflinching honesty and total lack of self-pity right to the very end.

Helen White (b. April 16, 1929; d. November 4, 2005): I would find within me the pluck, fortitude, and faith that carried you to the very ends of the Earth in the seventh decade of your life.

Thank you for all you gave, all you shared.

ACKNOWLEDGMENTS

I'd like to thank my sister, Leigh Leonard, for all of her support and encouragement on my long voyage toward becoming a writer. This book was her idea. I'd also like to thank my parents, Joyce and Harsey Leonard, for raising me to value experiences over material possessions, character over conformity. I appreciate their assistance in deciding which columns to include and their help with editing. Thanks also to Bruce Atkins for giving me the courage to become a writer and setting me on the path I will spend the rest of my life traveling. And, finally, thanks to the staff of International Marine for believing in this book and to Jon Eaton, Molly Mulhern, and Ben McCanna for challenging me with their insightful comments and thorough editing.

All but one of these pieces first appeared in *Blue Water Sailing* as monthly columns in a series called Blue Horizons. They ran on the last page of the magazine from September 1999 to October 2005. I'd like to thank George Day for giving me the opportunity to write the column and a free rein to say what I wanted to say. Thanks also for permission to use the name of the column for the title of this book.

Evans, there is so much to thank you for, I don't know where to begin. Let me just say I am honored to be your partner, in life and in our voyaging. I look forward to many more adventure-filled, challenging, rewarding years together.

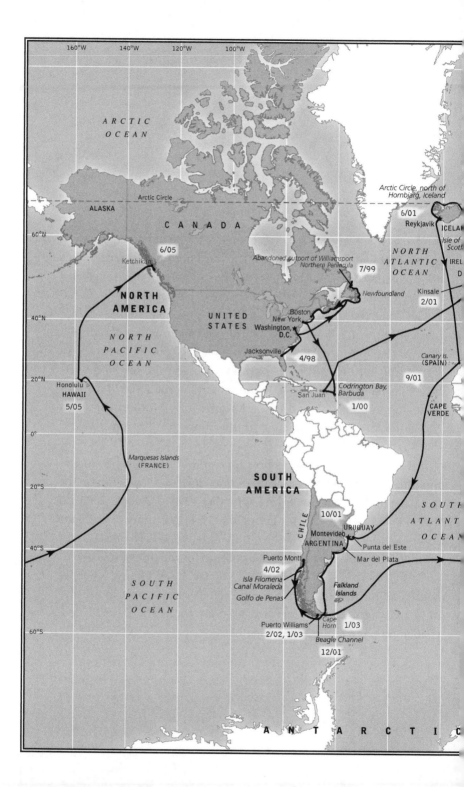

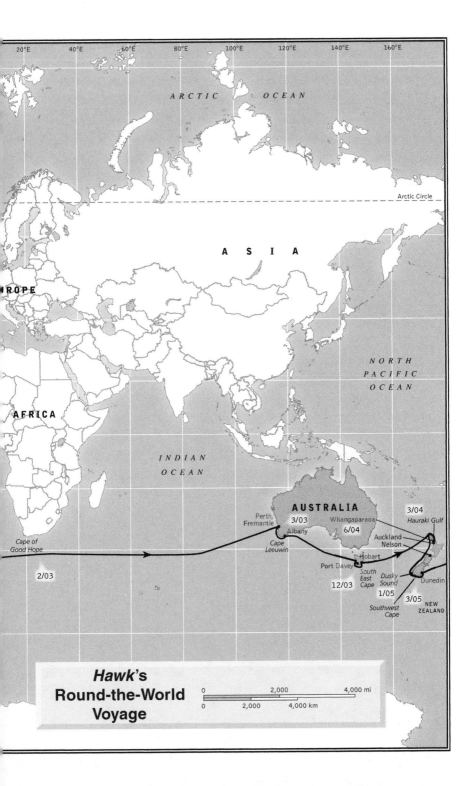

INTRODUCTION

At the end of Memorial Day weekend in May 1995, my partner, Evans Starzinger, and I sailed our 37-foot Shannon ketch, *Silk*, under the Newport Bay Bridge to enter Narragansett Bay, in Rhode Island. We sailed in company with dozens of other boats heading back to their berths after a pleasant day on the water or a holiday weekend at Block Island. But we were returning from a bit farther afield. We had last seen that bridge three years less three days before, when we set sail for Bermuda at the start of a circumnavigation of the globe.

Our voyage had spanned 36,000 nautical miles, thirty-five countries, and three continents. Our literal voyage measured in miles and landfalls was accompanied by a figurative voyage that tore up our roots; challenged our values; and tested our boat, our relationship, and our deepest selves. The literal voyage was written in *Silk*'s salt-scrubbed toe rail and battered dinghy, in our deep tans and the fine wrinkles around our eyes. But the real voyage was written in our hearts, and on that day we did not begin to understand how irrevocably we had been changed by it.

A few weeks later, when we said good-bye to *Silk* and left her to her new owners, we really believed we were finished with offshore voyaging. We both thought we could simply turn the page and move on to a new chapter. By October of that year, Evans was working in strategic planning for General Electric and I had started writing. But after three years of cruising, life ashore seemed dull, monochrome. Something was missing. The words for the things we had found sailing the world's oceans sound trite, almost clichéd: self-reliance, belief in humanity, trust in each other, respect for the natural world, confidence in ourselves . . .

Beyond these words lay the reality of who we had become. When we got back from our voyage, we kept being asked, "What do you do?" Before we left, we had never noticed how quickly people pigeonholed us based upon our occupation. From the answer to that simple question, most people assumed they knew what schools we had gone to, what neighborhood we lived in, how much money we made—even our political leanings.

Yet for most of us, the accident of what we do for a living has almost nothing to do with who we are as people. Whenever we arrived in a foreign port and met others on their cruising boats, we would often go weeks or months before finding out what they had done in their previous lives—if we ever found out at all. It simply didn't matter. What mattered was that they were there, in a foreign port, having had the will and determination to get there on their own vessel and brave the challenges along the way. That said far more about them than the occupation they had left behind.

When we got back from our voyage and got asked, "What do you do?" we literally could not answer the question. Better to ask who we were. I had become a sailor and a writer. Neither were "what I did"; both defined me as an individual. After a few short months ashore, I knew I needed to go back to sea to be true to both. And so we began to plan a new voyage and set about finding another boat.

We had left on our first voyage in search of the tropical paradise pictured on glossy magazine covers and in colorful sailboat advertisements. Yet we had most enjoyed the places we had visited in the temperate latitudes, not the tropics. In the

Azores, New Zealand, and South Africa, we had delighted in the diversity of cultures, the abundance of wildlife, the friendliness of the people, and the beauty of the land. We dreamed of cruising Scotland and Ireland, British Columbia and Alaska, New Zealand and Tasmania. But it was the thousand-mile-long archipelago of fjords and inlets, islands and channels starting at Cape Horn and running north along Chile's west coast that exerted an almost magnetic pull on us.

It took us four years to build and outfit a 47-foot aluminum Van de Stadt Samoa sloop, which we named *Hawk*. We had the hull welded in Florida, then we sailed the boat to the Chesapeake Bay, where we put in the interior. That project proved more demanding and difficult than sailing around the world. The image of the snow-covered Andes mountains dropping right into the sea, and glaciers calving into the heads of long fjords, kept us going long after we would otherwise have quit.

In the end we came through it, still together and with a boat capable of taking us anywhere on the planet. We built her strong to withstand groundings in uncharted fjords and ice-choked channels off calving glaciers; we kept her simple to minimize the need for spare parts and repairs in remote places without chandleries or boatyards; we made her comfortable for cold, damp climates by installing three inches of foam insulation and an oversize, bulletproof diesel heater. And yet when she was complete, we still didn't know if we liked cold-weather sailing.

To find out, we embarked on three summer seasons in the high latitudes of the North Atlantic, starting in June 1999. During that time, we learned the skills that would be necessary for the high southern latitudes. By July 2001, we and the boat were as ready as we could be for the Patagonian channels. We made the long voyage down the length of the Atlantic, sailing from Iceland to the tip of South America—from 63° N to 55° S—in a bit over four months. We spent eighteen months in Chilean Patagonia, cruising north to Puerto Montt at 42° S, then back south to the Beagle Channel and Cape Horn.

Having achieved our goal, we weren't yet ready to end our voyage. There were still places we wanted to visit, none of them easy to reach from where we were.

After much deliberation, in January 2003 we embarked on a nonstop, sixty-day eastabout passage through the Southern Ocean from the Beagle Channel to Fremantle, on the southwest corner of Australia. After a year cruising the south coast of Australia and Tasmania, and another year cruising New Zealand's North and South Islands, we made the 8,500-mile voyage catty-corner across the Pacific to British Columbia, arriving in June 2005. In six years, we have sailed *Hawk* some 50,000 nautical miles—almost half again as far as we sailed in *Silk*—and we have still not completed our second circumnavigation.

So . . . why? Why did we go, and why did we have to go again?

This book attempts to explain what we found out there, what we had to go back to sea to find again. But more than that, this book is about dreams. It's about setting your sights on a goal, then turning that abstract vision into something real and tangible. It's about pulling your dream over the horizon to you, one sail change, one course correction at a time. It's about living your dreams, dealing with their discomforts and disappointments while celebrating their magic and milestones. It's about going somewhere and—once in a while, for a few minutes or a few hours—getting there.

Chesapeake Bay to Newfoundland
7th day of passage

June 11, 1999

I HAVE finally arrived. The rising sun sets fire to each wave, a blaze of shimmering light stepping toward me where I stand on *Hawk*'s bow, until we too are engulfed, aflame. I have become porous. Emotion has become thought, thought has become being. The world is in me and I am in it. Sea time, passage mind. Home.

Three weeks ago, the rumble of *Hawk*'s engine reached me halfway down the dock. I had just exchanged my car for an envelope full of cash, disposing of the last physical possession binding us to land. With each step down the dock, I wrote the final words in a chapter of my life. The crossroads, so long in view, had been reached. Through hundreds of decisions over the past four years, Evans and I had chosen sea over shore, wings over roots, experience over convenience. Yet the sight of the docklines doubled back to the boat around the pilings made the money burn in my clenched fist. I wanted to run back down the dock and reclaim my car.

We put those six docklines on those pilings at Cypress Marine, off the Magothy River in the Chesapeake Bay, more than a year ago. They represented a promise. At that time our new boat was little more than an aluminum skeleton being welded together in a mangrove swamp in Florida. Evans wrapped each line around the piling twice to prevent chafe, then tied it off with a bowline. He secured the ends of the bowline with whipping twine and screwed plastic-coated red metal hangers into each piling to hold the neat coils of braided white line.

When we arrived from Florida after a 700-mile offshore passage and tied our new 47-foot Van de Stadt sloop into her slip for the first time, she looked like a finished boat. But down below, her aluminum ribs protruded through three inches of insulation into what was little more than a cave.

Over the course of the following summer and fall, we worked to cover her ribs and turn that cave into a home. When we could tidy things up, we took her sailing, but when saws and drills were scattered around the interior and ash boards were piled along her hull sides, we sometimes motored to a nearby anchorage and sat on deck under the stars, talking of landfalls to come. We always returned to that slip and those docklines. I marked each one with indelible ink so I would know exactly where to cleat it off as Evans backed *Hawk* into her berth. We eased the springlines to drop her stern to the dock when we carried the icebox and diesel heater aboard; we tightened them to hold her stern well off the dock after we installed the windvane.

For the first time in more than a year, three of those lines had been removed from their pilings and lay coiled on deck; the others had been doubled back to *Hawk*'s cleats. Evans motioned impatiently. I looked at the envelope in my hand, then turned to see my car pulling out of the boatyard. I climbed on board.

We stowed the docklines in a canvas bag, and Evans put them in the engine room. Over the next ten days, we worked our way down the Chesapeake, and I saw those lines every time I checked the batteries or turned on the solenoid for the stove. They comforted me as I struggled with vague misgivings, half-formed what-ifs, hazy might-have-beens, and unspoken regrets.

Five days out from Norfolk, just off Georges Bank, a forecasted 25-knot front arrived as a proper gale. The northeast wind lashed out at us, blowing from the exact bearing of our Newfoundland landfall. In less than an hour, the bottom leaped up from 2,000 meters to 500; the sea temperature dropped from 70 degrees to 54. Pinched by the bottom, tortured by the wind, confused by its own thermal energy, the frenzied water wrestled with itself. *Hawk*'s bow chased short, steep waves straight toward the sky, then crashed downward when they rushed by, throwing up huge sheets of water on either side. Green seas and white foam washed down the decks past the mast, but they couldn't reach me where I stood on the top step of the companionway under the hard dodger. The sea, the wind—even *Hawk*—paid not the slightest bit of attention to me. I felt small, naked, and powerless.

The turbulent sea matched the turbulence of my thoughts during the weeks just past. Had we made the right choice in leaving our careers, our families, and our friends yet again in search of what we so valued on our earlier voyage? Hadn't we learned everything the sea had to teach over the course of a three-year circumnavigation? Was life out here really so much more vivid than life ashore? Did we really find a more natural balance and develop more sustaining values over the course of our last trip? Had our relationship been strengthened as much as I'd thought? I'd believed it once. I'd encouraged others to chase their own dreams. I'd invested all of myself in this boat and this voyage. And now I couldn't find the magic I remembered so well and needed so much. When I closed the hatch and glanced aft into the engine room, I saw the docklines in their bag and felt betrayed.

But now, in the aftermath of the gale, as the rising sun sets fire to the slow-heaving silver sea and envelops me where I stand on *Hawk*'s bow, all of my fears and trepidations fall away. After seven days at sea, I have arrived. I have been scrubbed clean by the stinging salt spray and the howling wind. The sea, the gale, the emptiness, the sky—they have once again shown me my proper place.

I'm just a person, vulnerable, insignificant, mundane. I'm one cell in a body; one drop in the ocean—I'm a miracle in a world of miracles. As I celebrate that reality, I touch the place inside myself where my destiny dwells, and I know that only when I have been humbled can I grope toward the divine.

For the first time in many months, I can hear the quiet voice of my heart, the voice so long drowned out by the clamor of shore life, the busyness of managing day to day. It speaks through the pulse in my neck, the rhythm of the waves, and the sighing of the wind. It speaks only when I'm listening, when I am open, unafraid, and able to understand. It speaks of the cost of dreams, their exacting requirements, their frustrations and heartaches—and their incalculable rewards.

My mental compass has spun and settled, pointing once again to true north. I am here, now, and this is where I am meant to be. I hold the world inside my head as the world cradles me in its palm.

I go below to the engine room, pick up the docklines, and stow them properly in the sail locker.

50° 21′ N, 56° 26′ W

Abandoned outport of Williamsport
Northern Peninsula, Newfoundland

July 9, 1999

TWO gnarled paws of battered rock at the bases of the thousand-foot-high headlands on either side of the entrance channel engulf us. A gusty westerly wind, accelerated to gale force by the pine-clad arms on either side of the half-mile-wide fjord, threatens to blow *Hawk* back out the harbor's maw. Ashore, fir trees sprout straight up out of the crevices between rocks, on land so steep that the trees' branches occasionally touch the rising slope. Where no trees grow, granite outcroppings separate scree slopes, twisting rivers of flaked stone with round boulders frozen in their midst. Small torrents of white water tumble through the fir trees, one cascade on either side of the fjord.

A month and 500 miles of coastal sailing after our landfall on the Burin Peninsula, on the southwest coast of Newfoundland, we've reached the Northern Peninsula. This thirty-mile-wide thumb of land juts upward out of the closed fist of the island province to almost scratch the bottom of Labrador. The mountainous spine of the peninsula drops to the sea in sheer granite cliffs or wades out in long headlands that straddle fjord-like harbors. As we enter Fourché Harbour, our first landfall on the Northern Peninsula, only the navigation light on the rocks at the base of the southern headland suggests that others have found their way here before us.

"Quite a contrast to last night's harbor," Evans shouts over the grumble of the engine and the roar of the wind. I nod agreement.

By the time we came alongside the wharf, cars were careening into the parking lot, throwing up dust and gravel. Half a dozen children waited to take our lines, and a dozen more raced down the road calling to friends and families. Doors slammed and dogs barked. Within ten minutes of securing Hawk *to the wharf, thirty of the town's 150 or so people had crowded aboard at our invitation, with more arriving by car and on foot every minute.*

We spent last night forty miles to the south and east, at Harbour Round, on the north coast of Baie Verte Peninsula. From outside the entrance we glimpsed a few houses clinging to rock outcroppings in tiny clearings several hundred feet above us. At the head of the mile-long harbor, a large wooden wharf fronted a dirt parking lot, and a ragtag assortment of buildings trailed off behind rugged rock ridges on either side.

By the time we came alongside the wharf, cars were careening into the parking lot, throwing up dust and gravel. Half a dozen children waited to take our lines, and a dozen more raced down the road calling to friends and families. Doors slammed and dogs barked. Within ten minutes of securing *Hawk* to the wharf, thirty of the town's 150 or so people had crowded aboard at our invitation, with more arriving by car and on foot every minute.

"If the wind swings into the north, you'll get a goodly swell," one fisherman pointed out gravely. "Lots of water on the inside of the wharf. Whyn't you let us warp you 'round?" Others asked if we had enough water, fresh bread, seafood. Again and again we were thanked for coming into Harbour Round, for tying up to the wharf, for letting people come aboard. The focused attention and all the offers of assistance seemed excessive and somewhat embarrassing, yet we've experienced much the same in every harbor we've visited over the last month. In the world from which we come, such unstinting generosity creates an uneasy sense of obligation.

Here in Fourché no one watches, no one will extend us hospitality. Two miles from the entrance, we duck into a small indentation in the north shore less than a hundred yards wide and only a half-mile or so long. Here, slightly sheltered by a high headland from the wind whipping down the fjord, lie the remains of the abandoned outport of Williamsport. While it still lived, no roads connected this tiny outpost to the rest of Newfoundland; no power lines crossed the rugged terrain to bring heat, light, and voices from the outside world. The community was as isolated as a ship at sea.

Now it resembles a slow-motion shipwreck that has yet to complete its downward slide. Two dozen ramshackle wooden buildings line the steep-to shores; all have broken windows and wood weathered past paint to silver gray. One house has slid off its foundation and rests at a precarious angle on the hill. Cod drying racks, called flakes, still sit at intervals along the beach, though many have collapsed into heaps of logs. At the head of the harbor, the cemetery's stones glow white in the sunshine, and above them a white steeple canted at a fifty-degree angle marks the remains of the church. Several dories lie abandoned in the grass; flowers sprout from the soil that has gathered in their innards.

The cove's bottom steps up in great leaps beneath us, from 300 feet to 200, to 100. We drop our anchor in 40 feet, and *Hawk* comes to rest with her stern less than a boat length off the half-submerged boulders at the cove's head. The sound of the chain running out rises above the wind and echoes off the cliffs along either shore.

What a stir we would have caused here had people still walked the rugged paths between these houses and fishing boats still lined the derelict piers. We would have represented light and life, news of the outside world, supplies and celebration. If we'd arrived with a sick person aboard or a torn sail, the townsfolk would have done everything they could to put things right, just as we would have carried their mail or offered them medicines, all without obligation. Unstinting generosity would not only have been expected, it would have been essential to their survival, and to ours.

The people of Newfoundland, people who now live in Harbour Round and Burin and St. John's, are only one short step away from these outports, and they still remember.

Casco Bay, Maine, to the Cape Cod Canal
Overnight passage

October 2, 1999

I T'S one of those nights.

The bow smashes down. Forty feet behind it, my sea berth drops out from under me, leaving my head and shoulders momentarily weightless. With a waterfall rush of water down the side decks, *Hawk*'s bow pops back out of the water, and my sea berth bucks up to meet me. Head and shoulders transform from weightless to weighty.

I ride the roller coaster with my eyes closed, willing myself to sleep. In two more hours, Evans will get me up; then I'll get no more sleep until morning. Except for a brief interlude before the waves built up, when I first climbed into my bunk, I've not slept at all. An hour's sleep so far, I think, hoarding that hour like gold. Two more hours if I can get back to sleep right now. I'll be all right on three hours of sleep. It's only one night.

We left Casco Bay, in southern Maine, at noon, heading south and west for the Cape Cod Canal. The forecast called for northwesterlies, but so far the wind has come from the southwest, straight up the rhumb line. Though it is blowing at less than 20 knots, *Hawk*'s forward progress accelerates that to 25 knots over the decks. The wind has kicked up short, steep waves in this shallow water, 6 to 10 feet high and much too close together for comfort.

When *Hawk*'s bow smashes down into a wave, a hole seems to open up in the water to receive it. The next wave rolls in and closes over her bow, then opens again as she bounces back up and out of it, shaking herself off. Water cascades off both side decks in huge sheets, washes back to the mast or just beyond, then angles down to the leeward deck. The pitching drains our forward momentum, forcing us to carry more sail than normal in these conditions. With one reef in the main and the full jib, we're sailing between 25 and 30 degrees off the wind, managing 6 knots, tacking to the canal.

My neck aches. At this angle of heel, I'm lying as much on the hull side as on the bunk itself. By stuffing the canvas pockets that line the hull with the three layers of clothes I'll need for my watch later, I've created a soft and almost level nest, but I haven't gotten my pillows quite right. I shift and burrow, push one pillow outboard and pull the other down to my shoulder. Better. I close my eyes and relax, opening myself to sleep.

My mind floats in that magic space between consciousness and dreaming. Disjointed images from a week ago, when my parents visited, come and go. We went to windward then too. Much more civilized though. My mom sits under the hard dodger, smiling over her blue slicker, relaxed and happy on her least favorite point of sail. My dad's driving, his six-foot frame rendered child-size by our four-foot-diameter wheel, his gray beard and blue eyes making him look like an old English sea captain who caught the wrong boat. We have the same sail combination as now—one reef in the main and the full jib—but there are no waves and slightly less wind. We race along at more than seven knots, less than thirty degrees off the apparent wind, with the boat heeled about fifteen degrees. "It's one of those days," someone says.

I'm aware of the very moment when I start the slow drift down the hazy tunnel that leads to sleep. Tension slips away.

I don't hear the wave or the wash down the decks. But the shower of cold salt water pouring into my bunk brings me back to consciousness in an instant and propels me up and away from it until I smash my head on the bunk above me. "Evans!" I yelp.

He's already here, standing in the companionway. "I've got it," he says, pulling the companionway hatch shut. It takes a moment for shock and disbelief to ebb, leaving my rational mind to figure out what happened. A particularly large wave must have washed back past the mast, reaching the small opening through the hard dodger for the main halyard and reefing lines. The boat's 25-degree heel to port funneled the water straight down the open companionway hatch and into my bunk.

I can hear Evans pushing a canvas tarp through the opening in the hard dodger, but the damage is done. I'm wide awake, wet, cold, and miserable. I swear I can hear the sea laughing long and loud as it murmurs and gurgles along the hull side.

I spend the next two hours chasing sleep, but not catching it. When Evans calls to me, I climb out of my bunk, woolly-headed and clumsy. For each layer of clothes I pull on, Evans pulls one off. "Anything I need to know?" I ask.

"Nothing's changed," he answers. *Hawk* crashes down again and we both stumble. Evans shakes his head and sighs. "Why did we build a boat that goes well to windward when I hate going to windward?"

Over the course of the next six hours of my watch, the wind slowly shifts into the northwest. I ease sheets, and *Hawk*—freed from the pounding on her bow—takes off. By the time the sun's soft glow edges up over the horizon, we're closing with the Cape Cod Canal. The wind has dropped to a restful 15 knots on the beam; the waves have all but disappeared; the weak, late fall sun carries enough warmth to have me shedding layers; and the pastel sky suffuses the gray water with a pink iridescence. Despite less than two hours of sleep, I'm wide awake and high on the salt sterile smell of the sea and the utter perfection of the day. Evans pops out of the companionway, his eyes bright, his hair tousled.

"Amazing how we can sail four months and four thousand miles and not have one of those nights," he says. I smile, because all that's left of last night are some wet sheets. And now it's one of those days.

17° 00' N, 61° 47' W

English Harbour, Antigua
Leeward Islands, Caribbean

November 19, 1999

For something like the fiftieth time in the last four days, the rich baritone voice of Jol Byerley, longtime resident of Antigua and emergency coordinator for English Harbour Radio, breaks through the chatter on VHF channel 68 to fill *Hawk*'s cabin. "All stations, all stations. This is English Harbour Radio with the latest update and some very important information on Hurricane Lenny. We ask all stations, marine and shore, to switch to zero-six."

I drop my book and jump up from the settee just as Evans materializes from the forepeak. He beats me to the nav station, reaches for the VHF radio, and spins the knob through a blur of beeps until the dial reads "06."

"All stations, all stations. This is English Harbour Radio with the current position and forecast for Hurricane Lenny." Evans turns up the volume as the wild drumming of torrential rain on the coach roof reaches a new crescendo. "As of eleven hundred local time, nasty Uncle Lenny continues to be stalled at 17.8° N, 63.6° W, or about thirty-five miles west-southwest of Saint Martin. Though it has weakened slightly, center pressure remains at 951 millibars with sustained wind speeds in excess of 135 miles per hour.

"This dangerous, category four hurricane has become trapped between a high-pressure system to its east and a trough of low pressure coming off the U.S. East Coast to its west. Ten separate weather models have been used to predict Lenny's likely movement when it 'wakes up.' Only two agree, and those two call for Lenny to move east-southeast toward Antigua. But let me stress—it could go in any direction once it starts to move again. On the other hand, the National Hurricane Center in Miami and the Antigua Met office both say Lenny could remain stationary for another two days, or even three. If it starts to move toward us, we should have four to six hours of warning."

Evans sighs. "The only thing worse than two or three more days of this would be four hours waiting for 135-mile-per-hour winds."

We arrived in Antigua less than a week ago, after an offshore passage from Bermuda, only to discover that a late-season hurricane was forming near Haiti. For the last three days, *Hawk* has been tied stern-to the mangroves in the upper reaches of English Harbour. During that time, Lenny dawdled its way from south of Haiti to its current position just off St. Martin, where it has been stalled for the last fifteen hours. Ever since Lenny formed, the National Hurricane Center has forecast a turn to the northeast, away from the Leeward Islands, but that has not happened. On at least three occasions, Lenny has tracked straight for Antigua. For the last forty-eight hours, we've been pinned on the boat by unpredictable squalls and thunderstorms packing torrential rain and gale- to storm-force winds. If it weren't for Jol's hourly broadcasts and the constant radio chatter among boats, we'd be totally isolated.

"Reports from Saba say they've been experiencing ninety- to one-hundred-mile-per-hour winds," Jol continues. "I've recently spoken to my daughter, who says St. Martin's gotten eight inches of rain. Many boats have been damaged in Simpson Bay Lagoon. Our thoughts are with everyone on Saba, St. Martin, and St. Barts, as they are subjected to the brunt of the storm."

So Jol has a daughter on St. Martin, a daughter he must be worrying about even as he works tirelessly to ferret out and pass along every bit of information on Lenny. The thought shames me. What are three more days of wind and rain in comparison with the devastation on those other islands? After Jol completes his update, we switch back to 68 and the radio chatters away, connecting us to the world beyond *Hawk*'s hull.

"This is the Dry Dock. We're open if anyone wants to come in and get out of the rain. We've got some games going on for the kids and some laughs for the adults. Everyone's welcome."

"Jol, if you lose telephone contact, we'd be happy to offer you the use of our satellite phone so you can stay in touch with the National Hurricane Center."

"This is Sun Yacht Charters. We've got three trained paramedics available if anyone needs medical assistance."

"This is Turtle Rock. From up here on the hill, we can see an incredibly black line of clouds approaching from the west. Get under cover and snug everything down—this lull's about to end."

"This is Bailey's supermarket. We're now open and will stay open until the winds get too strong. We've got some fresh fruit, a few vegetables, and lots of bread."

"To those of you with friends or relatives in Jolly Harbour, the marina is experiencing heavy swell, but so far no boats have been damaged."

That tenuous voice link—from boat to boat, boat to business, business to house, house to boat—binds all of us on the island into a unique community. Faceless voices arranged more than a hundred boats in the mangroves of English Harbour with minimal coordination, fuss, or fighting; found anchors, lines, and chain when a catamaran arrived with only one anchor and rode; organized a tow and a dozen offers of medical assistance within minutes after another catamaran hit the rocks coming into Falmouth Harbour and one of the crewmembers suffered a head injury. We may be isolated, but we aren't alone. Other people are here who care, who will try to help, just as we will help however we can.

Two nights later, with Lenny a disorganized mass of thunderstorms heading out into the Atlantic east of Antigua, a group of more than sixty people gathers at the Admiral's Inn in English Harbour. I stand with Evans on the terrace, beer in hand, waiting for the guest of honor. Over the course of the last five days, Hurricane Lenny has battered the Caribbean islands from Haiti to Antigua; its storm seas and huge swell have wreaked havoc south to Martinique, Bequia, Grenada, and Bonaire.

Jol Byerley walks into the bar to a rousing ovation, wild cheering, and a spirited rendition of "For he's a jolly good fellow!"

Virtually the entire Caribbean came to a standstill as "Wrong-way" Lenny defied all the computer models and forecasts. But the storm hasn't defeated the island residents. Airports, restaurants, and shops are operational on Antigua and nearby islands. Wrecked boats are being hauled off the shore in St. Martin. Mudslides have been cleared from the roads around Antigua. Those made homeless have found temporary shelter, and materials are already arriving to rebuild damaged buildings.

As the singing winds down, the warmth in my chest and the tightness in my throat catch me by surprise. We move into the bar, and I lift my glass to Jol and to all the other people behind the voices that brought us hope and kept us from facing Lenny alone.

Mystic Seaport, Connecticut

December 14, 1999

W HAT'S it really like?" Serious dark brown eyes gaze at me from under black bangs with just a trace of gray; smile lines bracket the corners of her mouth; elegant eyebrows bunch inward, pushing up a furrow above her nose. "How can I possibly know if I want to give up everything to go cruising? How can I be sure I'll like it? How can I be sure my husband and I will get along?"

The last of the audience drifts toward the doors while I pack up my slide carousels. Her questions make me put down the box I've just picked up. Something about her voice, her carriage, or just her questions takes me back eight years—before *Hawk*, before *Silk*, before sailing. It is not a memory that surfaces, but a sudden rush of emotion: I inhabit my old self, see the world from an almost forgotten perspective, relive those painful misgivings. I almost feel as though I can speak to my past self through those earnest brown eyes regarding me with trepidation and longing.

But what words could I have understood then, before the challenges and rewards of cruising had so changed me?

When I don't answer, she says, "We've done all the sailing courses and seminars. We've had a boat for years and sailed it almost every weekend. I know I can sail—I enjoy sailing. But I don't think sailing has that much to do with it. I just can't picture what it will really be like."

"I couldn't picture it either." She studies my face while I put my thoughts in order. "I had no idea what activities would bind one day to the next. I could only come up with freeze-frame moments with subtitles like 'Cooking in the Galley' or 'Sail Handling.' I knew what I'd be doing if I stayed ashore. I could easily picture the life I was giving up. But I had to trade that for . . . what? A blank, an unknown. How could I ever make such a decision?" A quick nod encourages me.

"Now it's shore life that seems odd and difficult to understand and sea life that seems natural." While I speak, I think of waking last night in a sterile hotel room, made antiseptic by recycled air and deadened sound. I felt cut off from the real world, as if some vital connection had been severed. I threw open the curtains and stared at the moon, but I might as well have been looking at it on a television screen for all the contact the double-paned glass afforded. A week ago on *Hawk*, I slept to the gentle motions of the sea, woke to the sound of a tropical squall, jumped up to close the hatch left open to catch the sea breeze, caught sight of the moon behind the racing clouds. What could be more natural? How could I have ever thought it odd?

Her dark eyes look skeptical. I try to explain. "What's it really like? I can only answer for me. For me it's . . . vivid. Intense. Technicolor. Ashore we strive for convenience, comfort, consistency. Most people live within a very narrow emotional band. But until we went cruising, we didn't realize that in cutting out the lows we'd also truncated the highs. After we left, we rediscovered the incredible euphoria of youth, experienced again moments that we would have been happy to have last forever. But we also had to deal with the moments when we'd rather be anywhere but where we were."

Those highs and lows had turned out to be addicting. When we moved back ashore after our three-year circumnavigation, we never did manage to settle back in to an emotional middle ground. Since going to sea again on *Hawk*, we've gloried in the most beautiful sunset we've ever seen—in Newfoundland—and suffered through five boat-bound days in Antigua while Lenny played hide and seek with the Leeward Islands. The one doesn't come without the other, and the sum of both satisfies us more than what we experience ashore.

"So if I don't always want to be on the boat, if I don't always enjoy it, that doesn't mean I won't like cruising?"

I smile. "No one loves it all the time. It would be too easy, then, and it's not easy. It takes tenacity and determination and a willingness to be uncomfortable some of the time. It takes someone who enjoys a camping trip even when it rains every day."

"But how can I know if I should go or not?"

"You can't. And if you have to know, then you shouldn't go. But I can tell you this: if you feel the need to make a change in your life, if you're dissatisfied with who you are and the path you're on, any amount of time spent cruising will head you in a new direction."

The sudden, startled recognition in her eyes tells me I have connected to something in her life. I think of myself eight years ago, certain I was heading in the wrong direction despite following the script laid out for me—college to business school to international management consulting. With each step I took, I was moving farther from the person I had hoped to become. By setting sail, I stepped off that scripted path. I've been writing my own script ever since.

What's cruising really like? It's marvelous and terrible and scary and exhilarating. It's not for everyone, but I wouldn't trade it for anything.

17° 33′ N, 61° 48′ W

Codrington Bay, Barbuda
Leeward Islands

January 13, 2000

Barely twenty feet off the beach, I stop swimming and feel for the bottom. My feet touch nothing solid, and I end up treading water while trying to keep my nose and eyes above the little wavelets being pushed out to sea by the strong easterly trade winds. Ahead of me, the swell rolls in to a perfect sand beach that seems to rise straight up out of the water. I swim forward another ten feet, then my hands make contact with a mixture of soft sand and coarsely ground coral and shells. A wave washes by me, throwing me up onto the bank, then whooshes down, tumbling me back into deep water. The second time I am prepared—I dig in my toes as my hands find bottom, and I scramble up the almost vertical bank, moving with the water as it hisses high onto the sable sand.

I climb quickly up the hard-packed beach to the tide line, where my feet sink into powder-fine sand six inches deep. I spin around in a slow circle, taking in the view: the empty beach stretching away to the south in a broad arc; the shallow, wind-tossed lagoon behind me; the narrow bridge of sand separating the lagoon from the beach I've just climbed; and *Hawk* sitting alone, at anchor in perfect emerald green water.

Not a soul in sight. I have the eleven miles of perfect beach on Barbuda's west coast to myself.

Suddenly light-headed, I gallop through the deep sand. I drop onto my back and make a sand angel, covering myself in the soft powder. I jump up and leap down the bank into the water, belly-flopping off the edge of the world. I turn and swim underwater back to the place where the waves climb the beach, then let myself be washed ashore and tumbled back, scraped by coarse sand, then caressed by the salty warmth of the sea. I launch myself out of the water once again and go skipping down the hard-packed sand, my feet making delicious sucking noises while the sea hisses and foams under them. I play "catch-me-if-you-can" with the waves, chasing them down the beach, then dancing just out of reach while they crash ashore after me. An hour later, exhausted, I drop onto the deep, soft sand and let it cradle my body while I close my eyes against the bright tropical sun.

Images from the last few weeks float lazily through my mind. We spent that time forty miles to the south, in the crowded harbor of Falmouth on the south coast of Antigua, anchored with a hundred or more other boats. Less than a half mile away, another hundred-plus boats sat anchored in English Harbour. In that Caribbean crossroads, we saw old friends and made new ones.

A couple of weeks ago, a guy motoring by on another boat called over to Evans, "Who built your boat?" When Evans turned to answer, the man shouted, "Evans? What are you doing here?" We first met Mike and Fenella and their two children during our circumnavigation aboard *Silk*. We spent time with them at every stop across the Indian Ocean and back up the South Atlantic, but we lost touch after we left the Caribbean. That night over several bottles of Mike's excellent wines, we relived passages we had made and shared stories of people we had known. Evans and I renewed our acquaintance with their children, Jade and Merlin, now eight and eleven, bright, clever, polite, and unusually mature.

Two days before that, we had eaten brunch at the Antigua Yacht Club and started talking to a sailing couple with a brand-new baby. The conversation began across an intervening empty table and ended with the four of us sandwiched together on stools at a nearby bar, watching the America's Cup race in Auckland, New Zealand. During the commercials, we exchanged cruising information with them. We described our favorite harbors in the Azores, where they plan to be next year, and they told us about the weather conditions on the South Island of New Zealand, where we hoped to be in a few years' time.

But after several weeks in Falmouth, we grew tired of forcing our dinghy through the flotilla tied to the dock. We lost interest in eavesdropping on all the VHF chatter and couldn't get excited about an invitation to cocktails in the cockpit. Jol Byerly's morning announcements after the weather forecasts stopped enticing us ashore. We were ready for some solitude, but we wondered if we'd be able to find it. "The anchorages are all full." "Everything's so crowded." "You can't get away anymore." We had heard it often enough over the past few weeks to start believing it.

I roll over, pressing my hot stomach against the soft sand and exposing my cool back to the tropical sun. Alone on eleven miles of pristine beach, I think of the photocopied articles I was reading before I came ashore. They chronicle the circumnavigation of the s/v *Hurricane*. Gerry Mefferd, the author, wrote, "Our turning toward the Central American route to the Panama Canal, although not so plausible as the more favorable route through the West Indies, grew out of an early conviction to stay off the beaten path and get back into the hinterlands as often as possible." Those words were written in 1934.

Here on Barbuda, we have rediscovered a truth we learned on our last voyage. Paradise still lies to windward—a few hours, a day, a week, or a passage away. Even today, even in the Caribbean, yours can be the only boat in the anchorage . . . if you're willing to work for it.

18° 19' N, 64° 57' W

Off Water Island
St. Thomas, U.S. Virgin Islands

April 15, 2000

FROM *Hawk's* side deck, I watch my friend Laila approach, racing across the chop in her charter boat's dinghy. The dinghy had rounded the breakwater at Crown Bay Marina a few minutes ago, and now its white wake churns through the whitecaps in the anchorage off Water Island, just south of Charlotte Amalie, on St. Thomas in the U.S. Virgin Islands. The excited buzz of the black-striped bright yellow dinghy sounds just like its namesake, the bumblebee. The sound bounces around in my head, merging with the questions I've been trying not to ask, the good-bye I don't want to say, the leave-taking I don't want to acknowledge.

We first met Clive and Laila six years ago on Christmas Island, in the Indian Ocean, during our circumnavigation aboard *Silk*. At that time, they were resuming their own voyaging aboard *Isa Lei*, their 30-foot fiberglass Van de Stadt Pioneer sloop, after a three-year hiatus in Australia to replenish their cruising kitty. Clive was born in Australia but educated in Britain; Laila was Danish by birth, though she'd lived abroad, mostly on yachts, for almost a decade. Over the next 7,000 miles and two oceans, a mysterious and subtle alchemy transformed our initial rapport into the pure gold of lasting friendship. In the five years since we parted at St. Helena, in the South Atlantic, we have sustained that friendship with frequent e-mails, monthly letters, occasional phone calls, and annual visits. During that time, Clive and Laila became skipper and first mate/chef on

Holga, a 60-foot charter boat, while we built and outfitted *Hawk* and returned to cruising.

Laila shoots past *Hawk*, then spins the wheel, skidding the rear of the dinghy around like a pickup truck on ice. She throttles back in the middle of the turn, and the dinghy noses up to *Hawk*'s stern with a soft thud. I look down into rich blue eyes set in a deeply tanned, round face framed by sun-bleached blond hair, and feel as though I could be looking into a mirror.

"Here's the paella. It's almost frozen." She hands me a large plastic bag sweating in the morning air. "It should last until tonight just fine, but you'd better throw away any leftovers." She gives me a quick, crooked smile, then looks away. Evans and Clive have chosen to avoid this moment, but Laila and I need it, no matter how painful it might be.

"Thanks. We'll enjoy it tonight, wherever we end up. And thank you for the last few days. It's been wonderful." We had decided to begin our Atlantic crossing from the Virgins in order to see Clive and Laila one last time. They had a week off from chartering while the local diesel mechanics overhauled *Holga*'s engine. Though they were busy supervising the engine work and preparing the boat for their next charter, we had spent mealtimes and evenings together. They spoiled Evans with videos and their VCR; they spoiled me with unrestricted hot-water showers complete with foot scrubs, body washes, and luxury lotions. We celebrated Laila's birthday a month late with cake, candles, and presents. We relived old memories, shared new stories, laughed at familiar jokes, and reveled in each other's company.

But now our time together has come to an end. We will be departing for Ireland within a few days; they have charter guests arriving in less than an hour. A change in the weather later in the day will make this anchorage untenable, so we plan to clear out of the U.S. Virgins and sail 25 miles to a sheltered harbor on Jost van Dyke in the British Virgins, where we will wait for favorable winds to begin our passage. We hope we might see Clive and Laila once more before we go. If not, none of us knows when we might meet again. It is the nature of the cruising life that we can never even be certain of our good-byes, let alone our hellos.

Laila hands up another bag. "We will see each other again before you go. But this is for you . . ." The ". . . just in case we don't" she leaves unsaid, and I nod, understanding. Laila pauses as if to say something else, then half shrugs and releases the toe rail. The engine roars to life; the dinghy goes from standing to planing in a heartbeat. I raise my hand and wave. Her hand comes up in a half salute, then she turns away.

I watch until the dinghy rounds the breakwater and enters the marina. Evans comes up the companionway but doesn't say anything, respecting my need for another moment of privacy. When I turn away from the marina and the dinghy's wake, he speaks. "Time to go?" I nod in reply.

As we motor out of the harbor, a procession of partings marches through my mind. All our leave-takings over the last year can be summed up in one moment that took place last fall. After spending several weeks with dozens of friends at the Pequot Yacht Club in Southport, Connecticut, we dropped the mooring line on our buoy at daybreak. White frost cracked and crackled underfoot as we moved around the decks; our breath came out in smoky wisps while our gloved hands fumbled with stiff lines. We motored past the lovely colonial brick yacht club surrounded by flaming orange and yellow trees, then down the winding river toward Long Island Sound, the first step in the more than thousand-mile journey south to the Caribbean.

Ahead of us, the river narrowed to less than a hundred feet around a sharp curve. A figure stood on the sandy bank. As we drew closer, I recognized our friend Walker Vought, the person who had introduced us to the Pequot Yacht Club when

we moved to Southport four years ago. He stood at the end of a lone set of footprints extending for more than a mile across the frost-blanketed golf course behind him.

Walker raised his hand as we passed. In that frozen moment, with only the thud of our engine to break the chill dawn silence, it felt like a benediction.

A blessing. Indeed, all of these people, all of these wonderful friendships, are the blessings of our voyaging. And voyaging takes us away again.

To dispel my bleak mood, I go below to open the package from Laila. Inside I find all the bath luxuries I've been enjoying aboard *Holga* for the last week: body wash, foot scrub, organic shampoo, and hand lotion. An envelope contains a note—"To be opened when you reach 35° N." I smile. Laila is coming with us after all, as are all our sailing friends who have known the bittersweet sorrow of good-byes . . . and the sweet joy of the hellos that follow.

55° 15' N, 05° 55' W

North Channel, Irish Sea
Just off Mull of Kintyre, Scotland

June 10, 2000

*H*AWK flies, wings outstretched, skimming across the water, racing the playful whitecaps. Behind us, Ireland has lost definition and receded, its hills reduced to a low blue swell rising from the green sea. Ahead of us, the Mull of Kintyre, the thirty-mile-long peninsula that separates the lowlands of southern Scotland from the "Highlands and Islands" of the north, has grown from a dark smudge to a bold green headland. I find myself suspended between the two, overwhelmed by the sense of completion and transition. After months of planning and preparation, three weeks of passagemaking, two weeks of coastal sailing—after some 3,500 nautical miles—Scotland lies within sight, within reach, just over our bow.

I am acutely aware of the perfection of this moment. We are balanced between wind and water, between traveling and arriving, between closing one door and opening another. I know this will be one of those once-in-a-season days that we'll remember whenever we relive our Scottish summer. We're riding a 3-knot current with 20 knots of true wind dead over the stern, the main to port and the jib poled out to starboard. After having been hidden by heavy cloud for the last week, the sun blazes in a porcelain blue sky, and waves flash emerald green beneath the turning whitecaps.

Six weeks ago we were in the Caribbean. Then we raised our anchor and sailed for Scotland. Now with the Mull of Kintyre rising from the Irish Sea, I cast my mind back to feel again the combination of trepidation and anticipation with which we set our sails outside the anchorage at Jost van Dyke after preparing *Hawk* for a spring Atlantic passage; the rhythm of the days as we fell into our passagemaking routine and land's concerns receded; the frustration of cooking and sail handling while close-reaching in twenty-plus knots for a week straight; the hours spent tracking the weather and the days spent trying to slow *Hawk* down to avoid a large storm system. I hear again the loud "bang" as the staysail halyard shackle blew up in gale-force winds, and I remember the moment when we decided to detour to Flores, in the Azores, to replace it. I conjure up the image of Fastnet Rock in heavy mist and drizzle, the battered white lighthouse clinging to the black rock rising out of a heaving silver sea. I relive the throbbing of the engine as we motored too many of the miles around Ireland to avoid foul currents. Behind us lies every single moment, every single mile of our voyage. Ahead of us Scotland beckons, promising to reveal her own special character once we cover these last few miles.

As we close with the Mull of Kintyre, the misty headland resolves itself into high hills, then into a landscape of convoluted folds and tucks, a wrinkled and unkempt topography so twisted that my eye cannot follow the line of one valley or ridge. Its weight overwhelms me; its presence humbles me; its reality exhilarates me. Like turning an idea into something tangible, we pulled Scotland over the horizon, drawing it to us with each sail change and each course correction, willing it to appear. We made it happen.

In this indelible moment, I am fully struck by the wonder of that accomplishment. So much of our lives ashore seemed either inevitable or accidental. This landfall is neither. We did it. We sailed *Hawk* here. It wasn't passive. It was one of the most decisive, active, self-determined things we've ever done. We controlled every controllable aspect of the voyage, and accepted the risks for the rest. We covered every mile. We lived every moment.

The sea joins this headland to the hundreds of other headlands on the dozens of islands and the four continents we've rounded aboard *Hawk* and, before that, aboard *Silk*. The sea's thoroughfares are open to anyone with the means and opportunity—but even more with the desire and the will—to outfit a well-found boat and develop the skills necessary to sail her on the open ocean. It offers a freedom almost unique in our modern world: the freedom to control one's own destiny and chart one's own course, to be utterly independent and self-reliant, to take the ultimate responsibility and accept the consequences without interference. The sea does not promise comfort or convenience; it does not promise anything at all. But in moments such as this, with the miracle of a long-dreamed-of headland on the horizon, the sea delivers an unparalleled sense of completion.

As *Hawk* rounds the headland and enters the waters of Scotland, the squawk of the VHF interrupts my reverie. "Securité, securité, securité. This is Clyde Coast Guard, Clyde Coast Guard, Clyde Coast Guard. For a newly issued gale warning for sea area Malin and storm warning for sea area Rockall, please turn to channel one-zero."

Evans laughs. "Welcome to Scotland," he says as he drops down the companionway to tune to the gale warning. The door behind us swings shut; our voyage from the Caribbean ends. Our Scottish adventures have begun.

57° 17' N, 06° 10' W

Loch Scavaig, Isle of Skye
Scotland

July 3, 2000

I SIT sipping my coffee in *Hawk's* cockpit listening to the soothing hiss and rumble of the thin plume of water that slips down the sheer black wall behind our stern and marveling at its perfect reflection in the still water. *Hawk* lies at anchor in a basin rimmed on three sides by the Black Cullins, jagged, dark peaks rising from 2,500 to 3,000 feet above us. Green flows of coarse grass and heather separate the dark gray and black rocks jutting up almost perpendicularly to form the basin's formidable walls. The cascade tumbles down in a narrow ravine behind us, twisting and turning in a gulch carved over eons, sometimes almost doubling back on itself. It ends in a jumble of boulders and rocks before seeping without a ripple into the calm pool in which *Hawk* lies. Above the ridge over which the white plume of water spills, the jagged black pinnacles of the highest peaks sprout out of ancient falls of scree to stand stark against the blue sky. Loch Scavaig, on the southwest corner of the Isle of Skye, has to be one of the most magnificent anchorages we have ever visited.

The night before we left the Caribbean to sail to Scotland, I woke from an uneasy sleep with butterflies in my stomach thinking of the North Atlantic's tempestuous springtime gales and Scotland's treacherous waters. Many of our Caribbean cruising friends had reacted to our plans with a mixture of puzzlement and pity. "Everyone goes cruising to find this," they'd say, gesturing with their glass of rum punch toward the teal

33

water, white sand beach, and palm trees. "They're trying to get away from heaters, thermal underwear, and dreary, damp weather. Do you really think Scotland will be worth it?" Most of them didn't even mention my biggest fears—navigating in opaque, rock-strewn waters renowned for strong currents, tidal races, fog, and frequent gales.

"Everyone goes cruising to find this," they'd say, gesturing with their glass of rum punch toward the teal water, white sand beach, and palm trees. "They're trying to get away from heaters, thermal underwear, and dreary, damp weather. Do you really think Scotland will be worth it?"

Over *Hawk*'s bow, a white backpacker's hut sits in the middle of a grassy meadow backed by more cliffs. Yesterday afternoon we beached the dinghy in front of that hut, then followed the path around the shoulder of the cliff and over the black boulders and flat slabs of rock in a wide, shallow stream. We hiked along the twisting streambed for a half mile to where it emerged from an inland loch set in a long valley. Alpine-like meadows of heather, grass, and wildflowers bordered either side of the loch; these in turn were backed by steep ridges of the same black rock as that surrounding our anchorage. Almost two miles away, at the head of the valley, the Cullins rose sheer from just beyond where the lake ended to form a stunning backdrop to the scene.

I feel as though we are alone at the edge of the Earth, and yet two nights ago we enjoyed a superb chamber concert with internationally renowned musicians in a castle occupied by the same family for seven hundred years. Castle Dunvegan's current clan chief, John MacLeod, hosts a summer series of chamber music concerts mostly for the benefit of himself and his family, but a few tickets are sold to passers-by. We stumbled upon this concert, featuring the clan chieftain's son, Stephan

MacLeod, and purchased tickets on a whim, not knowing what to expect.

When we passed through the massive front doors into the medieval entrance hall, the laird of the castle, Clan Chief John MacLeod himself, stood on the bottom step of the wide, red-carpeted ceremonial staircase to greet us. Our host wore a white dress shirt, red cummerbund, and black tuxedo trousers and sported a magnificent mane of white hair. He welcomed us to his home and directed us to the drawing room. Fifteen-foot-high white ceilings and salmon-colored walls, decorated with a variety of oil paintings of clan members from different centuries, greeted us as we entered this intimate rectangular room about the size of a large living room. The Fairy Flag, a clan talisman dating from the fifth or sixth century AD, had place of honor centered on one long wall.

The musicians in the drawing room represented six nationalities. All of them, including John MacLeod's son, had trained in the very best conservatories in Paris, Cologne, and Amsterdam. They all had busy performance and recording schedules, and had performed with the symphony orchestras of most major cities in Europe. They came to the castle as John MacLeod's guests, bringing their spouses and children for a summer holiday. In return, they quite literally sang for their supper. I could hardly imagine where else we could have seen such world-class performers in a salon setting where we could experience every expression and catch every gesture.

It was approaching midnight when our host saw us out. The setting sun had colored the islands and the skerries in the loch in shades of blue while sending sheets of flame across the still water where *Hawk* waited at anchor. What a magical evening! As we walked back to the dinghy I felt like Cinderella at midnight, only my coach had turned back into a dinghy and my horses into oars.

ADMIRING Loch Scavaig while sipping my coffee, I sort through other images from our summer so far: the spirited highland dancing in which everyone joins whether age eight or eighty; the skirl of bagpipes from a neighboring boat in a crowded marina; evenings as guests aboard Scottish yachts critically sampling a wee dram of yet another fabulous single malt whiskey; visits to tiny community craft centers in search of handmade Harris tweed and Scottish woolens . . .

Evans climbs the companionway steps to join me, yawning and rubbing his eyes. "You're up early," he says.

"Just thinking about all those poor people in the Caribbean," I tell him.

51° 42′ N, 08° 31′ W

Kinsale, County Cork
Ireland

October 17, 2000

THE taxi brakes and slows as it negotiates the hairpin bend on the steep incline leading into Kinsale, in County Cork, Ireland. I strain for my first sight of the yacht club docks as we descend the last hill and emerge on the main street that runs around the head of the harbor. The forest of masts appears first, rising above a point of land beyond the round-bilged fishing boats lying on the muddy bottom exposed by low tide. I pick out the fractionally rigged mast standing a third again higher than any of the others, and in another tenth of a mile *Hawk*'s familiar silver hull emerges beneath it, shining in the low, slanting sunlight of a fall afternoon.

We arrived in Kinsale in September after three months in Scottish waters, just in time to settle *Hawk* into her winter berth before I caught a flight back to the United States for the fall boat shows. The last six weeks have been a whirl of sailboat testing, speaking engagements, catching up with friends and family, buying boat bits, and seeing to matters legal, financial, and medical. Now—finally—I'm almost home.

The taxi turns left onto Kinsale's busy shopping street and slows to walking pace while pedestrians dodge among the cars. I hardly notice the pleasing palette of blues, greens, and pinks on the buildings surrounding me, or the graceful old churches straddling the bright green hills beyond the center of town. After almost twenty-four hours of flights and layovers and delays and customs checks and immigration lines, I have reached the limit of my endurance. I want to unpack my bags and put everything exactly where it belongs, end the chaos and confusion of luggage living and return to the pleasing orderliness of the boat. I want to see Evans, to share all I have seen and done while in the States, to catch up on the racing and boat work he's done in my absence. I need Evans's help to put the bustle and busyness of my trip into perspective and find again the essential rhythm of our lives. While Evans and I have been apart, I have lived with a curious duality: I feel both strong and independent and less than half of a whole.

Reaching this point in our relationship seems a miracle of sorts. Take two type-A overachievers who both know they are right all of the time. Squeeze into a space smaller than most studio apartments, and regularly reduce sleep to one-third normal levels; add copious amounts of water, shake well. Expose to stressful situations. Bake for months at a time. Freeze occasionally. Not a recipe one would think would lead to domestic tranquility. And it didn't for us, not for a long time.

When we first left aboard *Silk*, we didn't really know each other at all. Our demanding careers as international management consultants allowed us to be together for a few hours on the weekends; we often went weeks without seeing one another. We spent more time together in the first four months after we set sail than we had in the entire four-year history of our relationship.

I had a wholly unrealistic view of Evans's capabilities and experience. I knew I didn't know anything about sailing, but Evans had, after all, been a charter skipper in the Caribbean and done an offshore delivery. Only much later did he admit that being a charter skipper had taught him little more than how to handle young men who—having failed to find true love, or at least a hot date, on their vacation—consoled themselves with an excess of rum punches. But I hadn't underestimated Evans's courage, his ability and willingness to learn, his intuitive understanding of things mechanical and physical— all qualities that ended up mattering far more than sailing experience.

Evans underestimated how unprepared I was to be alone with myself, how completely I defined myself through my job and my interactions with others. I am an extrovert by nature. Evans is not. Left to his own devices, Evans would revert to hand signals and dispense with verbal communication entirely. But I have to have some human interaction each day to maintain my grip on reality and my sense of self. So after our first offshore passage, I instituted a strict passage policy of one meaningful conversation a day of at least twenty minutes' duration on a topic of his choice. Gradually these went from forced discussions of some BBC news item with one eye on the clock to spirited two- to three-hour explorations of the differences between Polynesian and Western society or the environmental impact we had ashore versus on the boat.

We had much to overcome during the three years of our circumnavigation. After struggling throughout my career to be the equal of any man, I had to accept knowing less than Evans and being told what to do while I built up my sailing skills. Evans had to get beyond his shoreside assumption that paying a premium price guaranteed a trouble-free product and accept that in the marine environment everything broke eventually. We both had to find ways to channel the ambition and energy that had made us successful ashore into activities that gave meaning and added intellectual challenge to our life afloat.

As close as we had grown and as much as we had changed, building a boat together almost undid us. After sailing *Hawk* from Florida to the Chesapeake without an interior, Evans viewed all further work on the boat as a compromise of sailing performance. His vision of a few beanbag chairs and a cooler clashed alarmingly with my desire for comfortable places to sit and read, a real office complete with writing desk, and a well-designed galley with Corian countertops.

Somehow we made it through that as well. And when we moved aboard, two years ago now, we moved into a different phase of our relationship, one in which we both cherish what we have while recognizing its imperfections. It isn't perfect, and it never will be. But we've learned to laugh at ourselves and to count to ten. We've learned never to "discuss" something before the tension has melted away, and we've learned to say "I'm sorry" and "I didn't handle that well at all."

The taxi draws up to the yacht club gate. The driver helps me unload my overstuffed luggage, and I pay him. When I turn back to the gate, Evans is there.

A few hours later I lie wrapped in Evans's arms, savoring the absolute darkness and profound silence aboard *Hawk*. A sense of peace and contentment envelops me for the first time in weeks. We have overcome so much, and we have accomplished far more than I ever dreamed. Evans exasperates me and challenges me; he supports me and criticizes me; he pushes me to become the person I had hoped someday to be. I have no doubt that our fascinating, demanding, difficult, exciting life will continue to test our relationship. But I wouldn't have it any other way.

51° 42′ N, 08° 31′ W

Kinsale, County Cork
Ireland

December 30, 2000

Evans and I survey the red boat tied to the outer pier. Mast gone, stanchions bent, side dented, bow scraped, starboard portlights stove in. For a boat that was run over by a freighter two days ago, the 35-foot steel cutter is in fine shape.

After a midwinter passage from France, the little boat and her single-handed skipper were less than ten miles from Kinsale Harbour when the freighter plowed into them. The big ship's bulb caught the yacht amidships and rolled her onto her side and almost upside down, then pushed her through the water for several minutes before some observant deckhand caught sight of her mast. That the sailboat's skipper was below at the time probably contributed to the collision, but almost certainly saved his life.

The lifeboat towed the yacht into Kinsale, and the incident was reported on the news. A thin trickle of people have been meandering out to the end of the dock ever since, drawn by the all-too-human fascination with disasters and near disasters. One such onlooker, an angular man in his mid-fifties with a shock of steel gray hair over an elfin face whom we've spoken to a couple of times in the yacht club stops beside us. He puts his hands in his pants pockets, rocks back on his heels, and says, "Hard to believe she survived it."

Evans and I make small noises of agreement. The man looks at us. "Doesn't it make you nervous to be out there?" He gestures toward the river mouth and the Atlantic Ocean beyond. "Seeing something like this, I mean?"

Evans shrugs. "This is the first cruising boat we've ever seen that has been hit by a freighter. We know a few crews that have had near misses, and we know of one boat that was hit and sunk. But given the number of sailing boats and the number of freighters on the world's oceans, the actual number of collisions seems surprisingly small."

"But you can't know how many boats simply disappear without a trace," the man says.

"You'd be surprised how quickly the word gets around when a boat doesn't show up after a passage," Evans responds. "And it doesn't happen all that often. When it does, the entire cruising community will be alerted through the radio nets to be on the lookout for the missing boat. Most of them show up eventually."

"But not all."

"No, not all."

I find myself trying to think of anyone we know who died while sailing offshore. Though I come up with the names of a half dozen friends of friends, I can think of no friends or acquaintances. Yet we must know close to a thousand people who have crossed oceans in small boats. We know people whose boats have been taking on water, hit by lightning, knocked down, rolled, and dismasted, yet they all made it safely back to port. Based on this anecdotal evidence, passage-making doesn't seem that risky an undertaking.

The man next to me pulls a packet of cigarettes out of his jacket pocket, taps one into his hand, and lights it. "It would bother me," he says, gesturing toward the little boat. "So many things at sea are out of your control. I wouldn't like that."

"Some things are out of your control," I say. "But I think far more things are out of your control on land. Whenever you drive a car, you're putting your safety in the hands of other drivers, at least to some extent. I'm a lot more nervous in a car on your narrow Irish roads than I am in a gale at sea."

Evans nods. "So often ashore we're passengers . . . nothing we can do if something goes wrong. But on the boat, we decide how much risk we're willing to accept, and we control most of the things that matter, like how good a watch we keep or how well the boat is maintained. Then, if something goes wrong, it's up to us to deal with it. We're active, not passive. And what we do almost always determines the outcome."

We're really not particularly adventurous. Compared to many people we know, we sail very conservatively and take very few risks. After we rounded the Cape of Good Hope in 1995 aboard *Silk* and were congratulating ourselves on our arrival in Cape Town, a Contessa 32 single-handed by a young woman came into the harbor. Jo Hunter had bicycled with a woman friend from Alaska to Tierra del Fuego, then found work in the Falkland Islands, where the abandoned Contessa was sitting on a mooring in the harbor.

Jo had never sailed before, but she bought the boat, and she and a man from the Falklands sailed it to Tristan de Cunha, one of a group of tiny islands in the Southern Ocean between the Falklands and South Africa. From there, Jo sailed the boat alone to Cape Town. She described constant gales, repeated knockdowns, and cold, wet clothes and bedding in the same matter-of-fact way she talked about walking to the grocery store. After we met her, she left Cape Town and sailed the Southern Ocean route to Perth, Australia, arriving under a jury rig after her boat got rolled and dismasted along the way. Jo was comfortable with a lot more risk than we are. But it's the nature of sailing that we can all find a risk level that suits us, and we can control most of the variables that lead to success or failure.

"But there's always the unexpected," the man says as he flips his cigarette into the water.

And there is. That's why *Hawk* carries a reminder on her bulkhead, a picture of a boat sailing among icebergs with the caption, "A ship in the harbor is safe . . . but that's not what ships were made for."

51° 41′ N, 08° 30′ W

Bandon River
Kinsale, County Cork
Ireland

February 23, 2001

*H*AWK bustles down the river, carried by the ebbing tide, Evans at her helm. The 400-year-old ramparts and layered stone walls of Charles Fort slide by to port, and the open ocean comes into view between the fractured cliff and canted headland that mark the entrance to the Bandon River and Kinsale Harbour. After five long winter months tied to the dock, I stand with my legs splayed against the unfamiliar motion while my hands struggle to make sense out of a salt-stiffened dockline.

The cold wind cuts through my jacket and the three layers beneath, and I shiver. I fumble a loop around the bedraggled line to finish it off, grab two others already coiled from the coach roof, and work my way aft to the cockpit and the shelter of the hard dodger.

I tumble my unkempt coils onto the cockpit sole, and clamber down the companionway steps before dragging them below in my wake. I am in the engine room when Evans shouts. "Dolphins! Lots of dolphins!"

I scramble back up the companionway and jump onto the cockpit seat. Fifty, seventy, a hundred dolphins surround us, porpoising in groups of three or four, and the sea speaks in the tongue of their sharp exhalations. The sun reflects off the water, and as the creatures break the surface it highlights the fawn stripe running from their eyes to beneath their dorsal fins and the olive green patch below it. I spin in a slow circle, and the water fountains and ripples in every direction with their fluid motions.

"Please, write to me about dolphins. Tell me about the phosphorescence." The lines from my grandmother's first letter to me after we'd moved aboard *Silk* nine years ago reverberate in my mind like an echo of her voice.

My grandmother, Marion Arthurton, died on New Year's Day this year. She was ninety-one years old and had lived a full and happy life. She spent her last few years in a nursing home while her body slowly wound down, and her mind with it. I said good-bye to her when I was back in the States at Christmas. She opened her eyes and pulled herself from the gray and painful world she inhabited long enough for a flash of recognition to animate her features and bring a smile to her lips. But tears ran down her cheeks, and I cried then, too—cried for all she had been, all I had already lost. I thought I had finished grieving weeks before. So why are tears pouring down my face as these gay creatures swarm around the boat?

I did not know my grandmother when we left aboard *Silk*. Her first letter to me took me completely by surprise. What did she know of dolphins or phosphorescence? She was my mother's mother, a small woman in an apron, bustling around the kitchen making meals for the seemingly endless parade of people who always turned up just in time to sit down at her table. Her deep faith and uncomplaining acceptance intimidated me. She was quiet, serious, religious.

But I did write to her, first about dolphins and phosphorescence, then about the people we met and the places we visited, and finally about the spiritual changes cruising brought about in me. I saw her at Christmas and found she'd collected all my cards and letters into a photo album. She had bought a world map, and we hung it in her living room. Each year when I returned for the holidays, we sketched the thin line of *Silk*'s progress on its surface. Her insatiable curiosity and insightful questions drew details from me no one else cared about. Halfway around the world, in the small hours of the dogwatch, I suddenly realized she was the last connection I had to her generation. All of my other grandparents had passed away, and I had never really known them. It became important to me not just to answer, but also to ask.

When I couldn't ask, alone on watch thousands of miles from her, I remembered. When my grandfather retired from a lifetime of fixing cars and sold his garage in the mid-1970s, he and my grandmother decided to live year-round in their summer cottage on Sandy Pond, a small inlet off Lake Ontario. In an upstate New York winter, the two miles of unpaved dirt road leading to their cottage lay under six- to eight-foot drifts of snow. They rode snowmobiles to the cottage, which they heated with a potbellied stove. All supplies were hauled in on a sledge pulled by one of the snowmobiles. My grandmother must then have been in her mid-sixties, but I remember her riding a snowmobile across the frozen water under a full moon.

At sea, under another full moon twenty years later, I felt the blood bond connecting me to that adventurous woman.

I spent most of the summer after we returned from our circumnavigation with her in Rochester, New York. Though she was eighty-six years old and her body was already on the wane, her enthusiasm and wonder were still virtually unlimited. She would plan a trip to a local park for a picnic, a tour of George Eastman House in the afternoon, and a visit to a laser light show at night, then be disappointed when we managed only two out of three. We'd get up at eight, then sit talking over breakfast until eleven. We'd rush around to go somewhere, giggling over how quickly we lost track of time. Over the course of that summer, I discovered a kindred spirit and lifelong friend.

The dolphins cavorting around the boat make me touch the raw wound of my loss: I miss her terribly. As the tears run down my face, the dull gray feeling of the past few weeks melts away. A sense of release fills me, a lifting up and a brightening. The expanse of the sea around me gives me space to absorb, to accept, and to understand.

I would never have even had her to miss if I hadn't gone sailing. Her friendship, those precious years, those wonderful memories, are one of the sea's many gifts to me. The tears drip off my chin and fall to the cockpit seat, and I make no effort to stop them. I will always remember Marion—my grandmother, my friend—when I see dolphins.

51° 36' N, 08° 31' W

Off Old Head of Kinsale
Kinsale, County Cork
Ireland

March 21, 2001

F OR the last time, we round the bend of the Bandon River, and the headlands open up to reveal the sea beyond. *Hawk* starts to lift to the sloppy swell left over from a week of gale-force easterly winds. The black-and-white-striped lighthouse on the Old Head of Kinsale comes into view; we have sailed to this landmark repeatedly with *Hawk*'s cockpit full of Irish friends during weekends over the last six weeks, but we have not passed it in six months. As the Old Head comes on our beam, our Kinsale chapter ends. A new year of sailing begins.

This coming year represents the culmination of all our preparations and planning over the last five years, ever since we conceived of *Hawk* and our next voyage. If all goes well, we will sail north to the Faroes and Iceland before running all the way down the Atlantic to the tail end of South America, where we will enter the Beagle Channel.

When we chose to winter in Ireland, we did so because it fit into the carefully laid out itinerary created when we commissioned *Hawk*. Unlike when we left on our circumnavigation aboard *Silk*, we were determined to know this new boat inside and out, and to test her and ourselves in the conditions we would encounter if we made it to Chile. On our first voyage, we set sail for Bermuda one month after moving aboard and less than five months after purchasing *Silk* sight unseen. In contrast, we sailed *Hawk* for close to a year before leaving the Chesapeake in the spring of 1999.

On our offshore passage to Newfoundland, we tested the boat and ourselves in open ocean conditions. Newfoundland taught us how to dress for cold weather and delighted us with almost daily sightings of icebergs and whales. Our trip to the Caribbean provided more offshore experience, and the passage to Ireland across the springtime North Atlantic increased our confidence in *Hawk* and ourselves. During our summer in Scotland, we learned to manage twenty-foot tides and strong currents. In wintering in Ireland, we had hoped to accustom ourselves to the sound of gale-force wind in the rigging and to colder weather than we had encountered to date. We achieved both.

In a normal winter, we would have been able to sail through the end of October, but the gales started in the middle of September and succeeded one another every two to three days. The wettest fall in 300 years brought flooding to much of England and parts of Ireland. We didn't see another high-pressure system until January, and that brought cold winds blasting out of the Arctic and below-freezing temperatures for several weeks at a stretch. Wales, Scotland, and parts of Ireland had record snowfalls; even Gulf Stream-warmed Kinsale, with its palm trees, had two inches of snow, enough to close everything down for three days. Through it all, *Hawk* proved a cozy home.

But as we sail by the Old Head, I'm not thinking about how well wintering in Kinsale fit into our long-range plans. Instead I find myself reliving the hundreds of scenes that defined our Irish winter. On weekends in January and February, when the high-pressure systems brought crisp, clear days, we joined the parade of Irish families and walked the two miles from Kinsale out to Charles Fort. Dogs brought us sticks to throw for them, parents pushed prams up and down steep hills, children ran back and forth from group to group calling to one another about some amazing discovery just up the road. We stopped on the way back at one of our favorite pubs, usually the Bulman or the Spaniard, to warm ourselves near the peat fire and listen to the burr of Irish accents. A couple of local men played mandolin and guitar and sang Irish songs, and we listened while sipping Irish whiskey with a splash of water or enjoying a pint of Murphy's, the Cork stout, not to be confused with Guinness, the Dublin stout.

At the grocery store or the post office, the staff knew every customer by name and made sure to ask after the daughter in America or the son in London. The old men leaned on their canes and described in detail their child's schooling or their new job while the gray-haired women pulled out photographs of the grandchildren. An invitation to lunch meant several hours around a huge table in a stone-walled kitchen warmed by a hearth or a diesel stove while our hostess conjured up homemade quiche or mushroom soup in front of our eyes. Time had little urgency and flowed more smoothly and with less fuss than in most of the places we have lived.

Though Ireland has undergone an economic rebirth, it has yet to lose the generosity and openness more common to countries where the living comes hard and communities remain closely knit. Many of our winter friends wondered whether "Ireland could stay Irish" in the face of so much prosperity. The fact that they wondered reassured them at least as much as it reassured us. In Ireland we found an approach to life and a pace more in keeping with what we've come to want and expect after our cruising. The Irish we met and spent time with this winter showed us how we might take that pace of life ashore simply by making room for people and time for sharing.

Lawrence Cove, Bere Island
Bantry Bay
Ireland

April 1, 2001

Okay—try turning on the light," Evans calls down to me from where he sits in the bosun's chair at the level of the first spreaders. I double-check the cleated halyard that supports him, then go below and flick the switch labeled "Spreader Lights" to On. Back on deck, I crane my neck to watch him play with the multimeter.

Hawk lies berthed at the Lawrence Cove Marina fuel dock. Located on the northeast corner of Bere Island, at the entrance to Bantry Bay, on Ireland's southwest coast, this cozy marina is tucked into a tiny inlet almost completely encircled by low hills. We tied up here yesterday after an exhilarating thirty-mile sail past Fastnet Rock and around Mizen Head in steadily increasing winds and poor visibility. We motored into Lawrence Cove to find flat water and no wind at all. Only the occasional slap of a halyard at the very top of our mast and the low moan as the wind whipped over the cove gave any indication of the gale raging outside. This morning we woke to bright sunshine and a gentle zephyr, and Evans immediately set about a task he's had to put off in the windy and choppy anchorages we've been in for the last week or so.

"Darn, no voltage here. Okay, let me back down."

With one hand feeding the halyard and the other hand keeping tension on the coils around the winch, I lower him as quickly and smoothly as I can. I have already taken him to the first spreader once this morning, when he removed what we thought was a blown bulb from the port spreader light. The bulb turned out to be in working order, and Evans has now confirmed that no current is reaching the socket. Down below, he checks the current where the spreader wire enters the base of the mast. "We have current here. The short's somewhere between here and the spreader.

"Take me back up to the spreader," he says. "I'm going to pull the wire up through the mast while you feed it in from the bottom. I hope the short is near where the wire exits the mast." I crank him back up to the spreader and open the sail locker hatch so I can hear him from below. I push a foot or so of the wire into the mast and he shouts, "Got it!"

Back on deck, I see him fiddling with a bit of the wire and examining the cutout where the wire exits the mast. Then he swings around to the starboard side and has a close look at where the wire exits for the spreader light there. After a few more minutes he says, "Let me down."

He is not pleased when he reaches the deck. "Norseman didn't use any chafe protection where the spreader wire comes out of the mast, so it chafed right through the insulation. I'd replace the wire, but the conduit is packed too tightly. I'm not sure we can get a messenger through. And if we lose it, it'll be really hard to run another wire. I'll have to splice in a piece of wire, then create some chafe protection and find a way to support the wire from above to make sure it doesn't happen again. I also need to put chafe protection on the starboard side before we have the same problem over there." And, as an afterthought, "I should have noticed this before."

As I crank Evans up the mast for the fourth time, I find myself thinking about how our attitude toward maintenance and repairs has evolved since we left on our first voyage aboard *Silk* nine years ago. At that time, we expected to pay for quality work, and expected things to work and keep working. We assumed that the marine professionals we hired knew a good deal more than we did about our boat and its systems. Every breakage or problem caused a minor trauma aboard; we expected the boat to be perfect and resented having to fix things. A great deal of the tension in our first year or so of cruising resulted from not knowing the boat, not having the skills to fix what broke, and having things break not once but again and again. Now we hire professionals only for jobs we lack the equipment to tackle, such as recutting the mainsail or regalvanizing the chain. Though we designed and built *Hawk* to be as simple as possible, maintenance, repairs, and upgrades form the undercurrent to our cruising life, the woof to the warp of sailing to new places.

Much of this time goes into minor improvements and preventive maintenance rather than fixing things that have failed. Over the winter Evans completely replumbed the diesel day tank to correct an installation problem that let water and dirt into the system. And we installed a 2:1 halyard on the genoa that allows us to get better tension on the luff and reduce the friction on the furler. Rather than resenting the work that needs to be done, Evans now derives a great deal of satisfaction from developing new approaches to old problems on board, and a strong sense of accomplishment when his solutions prove themselves over several thousands of miles of real-world cruising. We still get frustrated when things break, particularly expensive equipment such as the instruments or autopilot, but we no longer resent it or expect otherwise.

We've heard it a thousand times and said it almost as often: "Sailing around the world means fixing your boat in a series of exotic ports."

As I lower Evans to the deck for what I hope will be the last time today, I add, ". . . and learning to enjoy it."

Off Nólsoy Island
Faroe Islands

May 22, 2001

Evans and I stand in the waist of the 100-foot-long gaff-rigged schooner *Norðlysið* (*Northern Light*) as she powers her way along within a hundred yards of sheer thousand-foot-high "bird" cliffs on the south side of the small island of Nólsoy. Above us, guillemots, fulmars, black-backed gulls, and puffins swirl in a blizzard across the brown stone splashed with long white streaks of guano. After a most extraordinary evening, we are on our way back to the *Norðlysið*'s homeport, Tórshavn, the capital of the Faroes.

About fifty people stand scattered around the decks dressed, like us, in multiple layers encased in foul-weather gear. Despite several hours in the persistent mist, penetrating drizzle, and less than fifty-degree temperatures, only a few people have taken shelter below in the *Norðlysið*'s spacious, well-heated main saloon. The rest remain on deck, mesmerized by the swirling cloud of seabirds overhead and the flocks of hundreds more floating all around the boat.

The Faroes, a remote and little-known archipelago of eighteen islands, lies almost exactly halfway between Scotland and Iceland. Its location made it an ideal stepping-stone along the traditional Viking route to Iceland and Greenland and led to its golden age as a trading center and provisioning port during the period of the Icelandic sagas, from about 1000 to 1200 AD. Since then, the islands have become an isolated backwater; their economy relies on fishing and subsidies from Denmark to support the population of 45,000.

Evans and I made landfall on Suðuroy, the southernmost of the islands, three weeks ago after an uneventful thirty-six-hour sail from Stornaway, in Scotland's Outer Hebrides. We found the islands more beautiful and the islanders less insular than we had expected. We were welcomed again and again by grave-faced men and pink-cheeked women who shook our hands solemnly after asking where we had come from and where we were going.

The owner and skipper of the *Norðlysið*, Birgir Enni, was one of those who befriended us when we reached Tórshavn. He stopped by with his family after church last Sunday and invited us to the *Norðlysið*. When we arrived, he gave us fresh mussels for our Sunday dinner—not the farmed or tidal variety but deep-sea mussels like none we had ever seen before. Their shells were twice the size of a man's fist, and their flesh was bright red and meaty. Birgir began chartering the fifty-year-old *Norðlysið* in 1989, and last year some 6,000 passengers boarded the wooden schooner for tours of the bird cliffs and sea caves on the islands around Tórshavn. We joined him and his guests aboard the schooner this evening for a concert in one of the sea caves on Nólsoy.

After motoring to the west side of the small island, the passengers and band members were herded onto small boats and transported inside the large cave. There the band played extemporaneously, harmonizing with the sound of the ocean sighing, using its rhythms to measure theirs. A saxophone led the rest, its sweet, golden voice resonating through the cave and echoing back off the walls until it harmonized with itself. The music had no origin but filled the cave from end to end, surrounding us, liquid as the water beneath the boat. After more than two hours, we emerged blinking from the cave, still hypnotized by the music and unwilling to break its spell.

Now we are on our way back to Tórshavn in the slowly fading light of a high-latitude evening. Near the southern tip of

Nólsoy, only twenty minutes from the dock, a shock like electricity runs through the people around us. Pointing fingers and excited cries indicate something over our stern. From his position at the four-foot-long tiller, Birgir calls out in Faroese that even I can translate, "Should we turn around?"

"Ja!" sounds as one voice from everywhere on deck. He pushes over the huge wooden tiller and we head back toward the bird cliffs. Ten minutes later Evans and I see what the sharp eyes of the islanders have been watching for some time–the high fins and narrow blows of orcas (killer whales) right under the cliffs of Nólsoy.

Birgir brings the Norðlysið within a hundred yards of the pod, then cuts the engines, leaving us to drift in the swell. The hundred people on deck are so quiet that we can hear sharp exhalations echoing off the towering cliffs to mix with the frenzied screaming of the seabirds. A sheer black fin as tall as a man cuts through the water surrounded by half a dozen short, triangular fins atop sleek black backs. A full-grown male orca more than thirty feet in length swims with his pod of females and youngsters. The animals move in an intricate and stately dance as they roll and dive, then surface again to swim over their companions.

The male orca breaks away from his harem and porpoises toward the boat, his white eye patch and gray saddle rising above the water with each stroke of his huge tail. A few oohs and aahs escape the crowd at his approach, and the whole group sways toward him. He comes within less than a boat length, not aggressively but curiously, then rolls on one side and looks at us as we look at him. After a moment, he dives and disappears until his fin reemerges among the still weaving, dancing group under the cliffs.

A few minutes later Birgir starts the engines, breaking the spell. The crowd shifts and moves apart as an excited babble of voices wells up all around us. As we motor away, I watch the circling fins and occasional blows growing smaller and smaller against the cliffs. Evans and I have been fortunate enough to see a half dozen species of whales from the decks of our own boat. The experience always moves me, but this time I am moved not just by the creatures themselves but by how they captivated every human aboard. I feel a sudden surge of hope for their species—and for ours.

66° 31′ N, 22° 32′ W

Arctic Circle, north of Hornbjarg
Iceland

June 21, 2001

Cat's-paws of wind ruffle the sea's calm surface and gently caress *Hawk*'s light air reacher and mainsail, ghosting us along through leaden Arctic seas. Evans's head and shoulders appear in the companionway, his face still creased from a pillow and his jaw shadowed by a day-old beard. "You should try to get some sleep," he says.

I nod. "It's clouding up," I tell him. Evans shrugs, but I see his shoulders slump as he turns away to put on his foul-weather gear. I scan the sky once again from horizon to horizon. Overhead, the wispy morning clouds have been replaced by a denser, more angular variety, and a broad band of darker clouds approaches from the west. The clouds have not yet begun to affect the supernatural, high-latitude clarity; with binoculars I can easily pick out details of color and texture on Hornbjarg, an antlerlike rock sprouting from a rugged headland a few miles south of the Arctic Circle, some thirty-five miles over our bow.

We are trying to fulfill a fantasy, one that began on a cold winter day in Ireland when Evans was route planning for the summer to come. "Do you know the definition of the Arctic Circle?" he asked me. I said I didn't.

"It's the northern latitude where the sun doesn't set on one and only one day of the year—on the summer solstice." He looked at me. "Wouldn't it be wonderful to be sailing exactly on the Arctic Circle on midsummer's eve and see that?" And the perfect place to do that, we decided, was just north of Iceland's Hornbjarg, the country's Cape Horn.

At that time, neither of us had any idea of how many things would have to go just right in order to live his fantasy. But in the month we have spent cruising Iceland, we have learned. Within ten days of our early-June landfall on the east coast, the temperamental Icelandic weather introduced itself with two blizzards packing storm-force winds. Clear skies regularly turned to overcast or fog in less than an hour. On the rare occasion when steady winds blew, they were shifted, funneled, and accelerated by the fjords, then snuffed out completely in the lee of high headlands. The few secure harbors lay twenty to thirty miles from the sea at the heads of meandering fjords, so our "day sails" averaged more than a hundred miles.

These are the moments we hunger for when we return to shore. These are the moments I would somehow capture and share with those who ask "why?" But such moments come only after the discomfort, the tedium, the fear. They come out of the challenges and the hardships and cannot be separated from them. For neither fear nor wonder are enough. It is the sum total of both that makes us whole and real and alive and keeps us out here, in search of more.

To be sailing along 66° 30' (and some odd seconds) north for several hours on the one day of the year when the sun would not set—and to actually watch it drop, then rise again over the course of several hours—would take perfect timing, calm weather, good visibility, and a good deal of luck. When we left Akureyri, at the head of thirty-mile-long Eyjafjörður, on the north coast of Iceland, some fifteen hours ago, we dared to hope. Now the lowering cloud cover looks set to spoil things at the last minute.

I mentally shake myself. We've enjoyed a day of magnificent sailing along Iceland's north coast, with its snow-capped mountains and plunging waterfalls. The rest will happen—or it won't. In the meantime, I decide to get some sleep.

Evans wakes me a bit after midnight. "Come see," is all he says. I clamber out of bed, and the chill in the cabin warns me of the temperature outside. I pull on my full Arctic wardrobe as quickly as I can, entranced by the incredible golden hue seeping in through the slit side windows. Within minutes, I slide back the companionway hatch and climb out on deck.

The sky has cleared completely. The sun lies just above the horizon due north of us, its long golden rays bathing everything in an evanescent glow. We passed Hornbjarg less than an hour ago and are making our way along the twenty-mile-long, shallowly indented coastline at the northern end of the uninhabited peninsula of Hornstrandir. Behind us, Hornbjarg's tortured rock outcropping rises several hundred feet above the barren peninsula. Basaltic cliffs bleed the red scree that backs a blasted black-sand moonscape in the bay called Hornvík.

A series of sheer sea cliffs more than a thousand feet high overshadow us, glowing rose, copper, and gold in the wash of the midnight sun. Seabirds rest on the water in large flocks, wheel overhead, and dive to rise with a flash of water from their wings, or swoop and glide several miles away in front of the cliff. Through binoculars, these farthest birds look like a blizzard of snowflakes drifting down across the red and black rock face.

In the course of the day, the sun has scribed a huge circle in the sky above us. Its slanting rays first streaked over the high peaks bordering the eastern side of Eyjafjörður at three in the morning, then it rose until it was overhead to the south. By the time I went below to get some sleep, it had dropped to the west until it was in front of us. Then it circled to the north as it descended, until now it stands due north.

The sun grows more and more intense as it approaches the horizon, turning from yellow to a blinding orange that leaves us blinking spots whenever we glance at it. The cliffs glow a deeper and deeper red, and the seawater becomes black and opaque. Eventually the sun touches the horizon and grows fat, then seems to hover there for about half an hour. We keep taking quick glances, unable to avoid the feeling that time has stopped and might never start again. After forty minutes we perceive a tiny separation at the horizon as the sun lifts skyward to begin a new day.

Even as the sun climbs and the magical sense of suspended time recedes, I know that this hour will live on in our memories long after our sailing adventures have ended. The birds, the cliffs, the light, the sluggish sea, the mist from our breaths— all have coalesced into a defining moment of this voyage and of our lives. These are the moments we hunger for when we return to shore. These are the moments I would somehow capture and share with those who ask "why?" But such moments come only after the discomfort, the tedium, the fear. They come out of the challenges and the hardships and cannot be separated from them. For neither fear nor wonder are enough. It is the sum total of both that makes us whole and real and alive and keeps us out here, in search of more.

Vestmannaeyjar, Iceland to Canary Islands
Landfall on 14th day of passage

August 5, 2001

*H*AWK surfs in the crest of a silver sea, bathed in a swath
of platinum laid across the water's surface by the wide white
eye of the bright full moon. I stand with one foot on each of
the cockpit seats, my hands gripping the grabrail on the back
edge of the hard dodger. All around us, the ponderous waves
kicked up by three days of 30-knot winds move like molten
metal, their surfaces churned into heaving and surging
wavelets glinting gold and silver. The desert sand carried on
the hot breath of the Sahara, only forty miles to windward,
shrouds a humpbacked island, Isla de Alegranza, reducing it to
a hazy silhouette though it is less than three miles distant.
After having sailed for fourteen days and 2,350 nautical miles,
this shadowy outpost of the Canary Islands welcomes us,
promising an end to the ceaseless noise and motion and an un-
broken night of deep and dreamless sleep.

How far we have come! Less than five weeks ago, *Hawk*
swung to her anchor in a deserted fjord on Iceland's north
coast, less than a degree south of the Arctic Circle. Snow still
blanketed the alpine meadows above us and lay in melting
drifts right to the water's edge. The soothing rumble of meltwater tumbling into the sea in a dozen small waterfalls under-
lay the "kea" shriek of hundreds of Arctic terns and the duck-
like muttering of huge flocks of eiders. In the supernatural
clarity of the pure Arctic air, the serrated edge of Iceland's
northernmost glacier, Drangajökull, had been clearly visible

as we entered the fjord, though it lay more than twenty miles to the south.

We had left Iceland three weeks later, headed due south—a course that would take us straight to the Canaries without sighting any other land. Unlike on a tropical passage, where the days can hardly be distinguished one from the other, and it takes the crosses marking our noon positions on the chart to convince us we're moving at all, each and every day we sailed south brought tangible evidence of our progress.

We left the Vestmannaeyjar, the small island group off the southwest corner of Iceland, dressed in thermal underwear, fleeces, sea boots, hats, and gloves. Neither moon nor stars were visible in the few hours of twilight that pass for night in the high-latitude summer. We each reefed and raised sail a half dozen times per watch as the inconsistent polar easterlies veered and backed, strengthened and died. As we drove the boat south, the short summer nights grew dark, then lengthened hour by hour. At the latitude of the Orkney Islands, I suffered the night terrors of a three year old when I went on deck at the beginning of my watch and, for the first time in three months, I couldn't see the bow. But a few hours later, I couldn't take my eyes from the phosphorescence surging across the surface of the jet black sea with each cresting wave like heat lightning pulsing on the horizon on a sultry summer night.

A few degrees south of 50° N, we knew we had left the high latitudes. We saw it in the sea color, no longer gunmetal gray but a deep, dusky violet-blue in the bright afternoon sunshine. We saw it in the clouds, grown puffy and soft and bleached white instead of hard and angular and the color of smoke. We felt it in the increasingly consistent winds as they swung from the eastern quadrant into the west, then returned to the northeast and built into trades.

But most of all we felt it in the increasing humidity and temperature. We stripped away the shrink-wrap plastic insulating ports and hatches and opened them for the first time in ten months. We stowed the down sleeping bags, then the wool blankets before pulling out the light cotton beach blankets we use in the tropics. We shed fleeces and thermal underwear, dug out long-sleeved shirts and light pants, then switched to shorts and T-shirts. Our first long, luxurious showers in the cockpit uncovered toes we had not seen for more than a few minutes at a time in months. Despite generous quantities of sunblock, winter-white skin on legs and arms turned pink, then red before beginning to bronze. Every degree we have traveled south toward this landfall has been evident in the weather and the winds—the very pulse of our planet.

Isla Graciosa rears up out of the quicksilver sea, the rolling sand dunes gold and yellow in the moon's light. Evans comes up on deck and we furl the sails, then start the motor to power our way the last mile into the anchorage between Graciosa and Lanzarote. The friendly light of another yacht guides us into the sandy anchorage we visited once before, nine years ago. The anchor splashes into the water and the chain rumbles over the bow roller after it. *Hawk* settles back on the anchor, and though the reinforced trade winds still howl at 30 knots, we're in the lee of the island and well protected from the boisterous seas.

I close my eyes and picture that anchorage just below the Arctic Circle, and I can hardly believe that both places exist on the same planet. At first it seems to me that only the wind roaring in my ears is the same. Yet when I open my eyes again and drink in the staggering beauty of the eroded volcanic cones and sand dunes painted in hues of silver and gold by the wash of the full moon, I see the uncanny resemblance to that other raw volcanic landscape of white snow and black rock. This passage has linked the two, tied them together with slow but noticeable changes in daylight and temperature, to encompass the unbelievable diversity and undeniable interconnectedness of our lovely, fragile, precious planet.

I recognize the feeling welling up inside of me in a great wave. This same sense of awe and wonder filled me when I stood in *Hawk*'s cockpit surrounded by the laughter of the snowmelt. I have felt it when gazing into the eye of a sperm whale, when watching the waves pyramid and collapse in a storm at sea, when marveling at the colors in a double rainbow. For I, too, am of this world and irrevocably connected to it, and when I get close enough to nature to sense that connection, my soul resonates with delight, fills with longing, trembles with fear, and soars with hope.

32° 13′ S, 49° 30′ W

Cape Verdes to Punta del Este, Uruguay
24th day of passage

October 16, 2001

I WAKE instantly and completely, every sense on high alert, aware of danger. In the split second before a waterfall-like rumble begins, I hear the muffled roar of 40-knot winds and the crash and whoosh of 15-foot seas, and I feel the tug of war between the storm jib on the bow and the drogue off our stern. Time turns to molasses as I lie on the bunk with every muscle in my body clenched as tight as a fist.

Then there's a terrific crash from astern. *Hawk* staggers sideways and down, and time leaps into fast forward as everything happens at once. I feel the sensation of free fall in the pit of my stomach, then my chest fetches up against the restraining strap above the lee cloth on the bunk as my knee slams into the bunk board. I see a solid wall of water gushing in through the opening where the top hatch board should be. A continuous roaring engulfs me before ending in several loud crashes from forward followed by the sound of breaking glass.

Time stops as this sound echoes inside my head. A pause, then silence, like an indrawn breath. My brain tries to catch up with my senses, and two thoughts surface above the seething maelstrom of my mind—one from my heart, one from my head—to emerge from my lips. "Evans! Are you all right? The glass in the hard dodger must have exploded!"

A dark shape enters my line of vision, and Evans's strained voice reaches me as he climbs the steps to the companionway. "A piece of the rig must have come down—that's the only way those windows could break!" I somehow go from lying in the bunk to standing in my bare feet in a small sea of saltwater in the galley. Every major muscle in my body trembles. I breathe in short spasms; my heart pounds; my hands sweat. Evans's flashlight beam darts around, cutting the darkness above me, creating a herky-jerky strobe effect below, like an old black-and-white film.

Time stops again as I realize there might be glass all over, and I look stupidly at the cabin sole but see only the glint of moving water. I become aware of my panting breath and tell myself I will *not* panic. We are both unharmed. I chant those words again and again in my mind, and time starts to steady with my breathing.

I have to *do* something—anything. I move into the main saloon, pull on a shirt and some waterproof pants, and start rummaging for large towels to sop up the sea on the cabin sole. I'm vaguely aware of drops of water in a spray pattern radiating outward from the mast. Water sloshes around on my writing desk and drips from the books above and outboard of it. A split second later my mind catches up, and I realize the wave that boarded us came through the companionway with so much force that it hit the mast fifteen feet away like spray from a fire hose.

A scant two minutes after he went on deck, Evans drops down the companionway steps, and the solid fact of him ends the wash of emotions threatening to overwhelm me. He looks haggard but sounds amazed. "The hard dodger's intact, and I can't see anything wrong with the rig. We lost the winch handle we stow in the dorade next to the mast, but everything else seems fine." I can scarcely believe it, but my mind much more quickly accepts this miracle than it did the disaster I had anticipated.

Two hours later, I stand on the top step of the companionway peering into the inky blackness, hoping against hope to see a freighter's lights before it closes with us in the driving salt spray and high waves. We have achieved some sort of order again below, and I have asked Evans why the top hatch board was not in place. "With the wind vane broken and the autopilot doing the steering, if we go below we have to be able to get out the companionway fast if the boat starts to broach. It takes several seconds to get that hatch board out and secure it."

I struggle over the same choice and worry over a hundred other things: We never found any broken glass when we cleaned up, so what broke when we were hit by the wave? Is the boat feeling comfortable and moving well, or has she started to get rushed off her feet? Should we drop the storm jib and run bare-poled with just the drogue? Will our autopilot hold up, or will we have to hand-steer for the last forty-eight hours of this passage through storm winds and seas? How bad will the waves be when we close with the continental shelf in a few hours?

From the sea bunk in the aft cabin below me, I hear Evans roll over, so I know he's awake. "You know," I say into the darkness, "a log cabin, a fireplace, a cat, and a garden sound pretty good right now." A disembodied chuckle rises up and caresses my ear before it is lost in the sounds of a storm at sea.

Yacht Club Argentino
Mar del Plata, Argentina

November 20, 2001

THE putt-putt of the dinghy engine echoes off the retaining walls on either side of us as we pass under the swing bridge that spans the narrow channel leading into the yacht basin of the Yacht Club Argentino, at Mar del Plata. I look back just as *Hawk*, tied to one of the industrial-size mooring buoys outside the yacht basin, disappears from view. We arrived at the resort city late yesterday afternoon after a thirty-six-hour sail from Punta del Este, Uruguay. Now, refreshed by a good night's sleep, we are heading ashore to go through customs and take our first look at the yacht club and the city.

Once through the narrow opening, we enter an almost land-locked lagoon filled with motor- and sailboats. Jetties extend into the center of the basin from all sides, creating a labyrinth of channels. The local boats tied to the docks are in the 30- to 35-foot range, but as we turn toward the white-painted yacht club buildings, Evans says, "Look! We've found the foreign legion." A Canadian flag, a Dutch flag, a French flag, an American flag, and a Swedish flag fly from the sterns of five yachts lining the docks along the main channel. These are all 40- to 50-foot-long, highly competent-looking offshore boats.

At the sight of these yachts, all so far from home, I feel a curious mixture of emotions—pride at their presence and their diversity, anticipation of new friends and shared experiences, curiosity about where they have come from and where they are going, and hope that we might see these boats again at future landfalls. These emotions, all once so familiar on entering a new harbor, now seem almost alien to me. In the last twelve months we have grown used to being the token yacht among the fishing boats, and I have all but forgotten the joys of being part of the larger cruising community.

After we've completed the formalities with the port officials, we introduce ourselves to the crews on each of the yachts. Four of the five boats are heading south; these will be our companions for the next six months to a year as we cruise the Chilean channels. Only the Canadian yacht, *Mist*, a 43-foot Cape George cutter that Lina and Jim Gallup purchased as a bare hull and fitted out themselves, is heading north, having already spent nine months in Chile.

Jim and Lina made landfall in Arica, just south of the Peruvian border, and cruised the entire length of Chile's 2,000-plus-mile coastline. They reached the Beagle Channel and Cape Horn in the middle of the Southern Hemisphere winter and arrived in Mar del Plata a few weeks ago, at the start of the southern summer. *Mist* has become information central. Jim and Lina invite us for coffee after lunch to answer all of our many questions about cruising Chile.

We arrive to find most of the other crews aboard, filling the spacious boat to overflowing. Jim is discussing Southern Ocean weather patterns around the standup navigation station with Evans Hoyt, the skipper of the American fiberglass ketch *Finnrose*, and Aad, from the Dutch custom steel boat *Helena Cristina*. Aad and Hella sailed to the Horn twenty years ago with their two children. They have returned because they "forgot" to do Antarctica. Lina sits at the main saloon table next to Gustaf, from the Swedish homebuilt steel yacht *Caminante*, pointing at the screen of a laptop computer that displays charts of Chile. Pierre, from the French Colvin Archer *Morgengry*, sticks his head down the companionway to ask Jim about SSB frequencies for the recently established Patagonian Cruiser's net.

The contained bustle feels warm and personable, and I have to remind myself that these people have known one another for only a matter of days. By the end of the afternoon, we too have become part of the foreign legion, and the seeds of new and lasting friendships have been sewn.

OVER the next few days, we spend most of our time on one yacht or another, getting acquainted and trading information on everything from good Internet weather websites to the best wine values in Argentina. When we get a forecast for four days of northerly winds, ideal for heading farther down the coast, we still need to complete some sail work before leaving Mar del Plata. But the other southbound crews have already been in the yacht club for more than a week and are ready to move on, so the favorable forecast has them running into town for last-minute provisions before clearing out. The planned early-morning departures slip into early afternoon as everyone remembers one more thing to ask Jim or one more e-mail address to exchange.

We return to *Hawk* around two in the afternoon, and the first boat comes through the swing bridge at three. *Caminante's* green hull has just disappeared out the mouth of the main harbor when the bridge swings open again and *Helena Cristina* motors through the channel. While Aad circles us, Hella calls, "New Year's in Ushuaia?" Finally *Finnrose* emerges, with Evans Hoyt at the helm. Becky and their Argentinean crew member, Pedro, stow docklines and fenders while we wave and wish them bon voyage.

As *Finnrose's* crew raises sails and heads for the channel leading out the main breakwater, I don't feel the usual bittersweetness of cruising farewells. This has been a prelude, I know, to warm friendships that will develop farther south, among a community of sailors who have chosen to wander fairly far from the beaten track. After a year of having beautiful anchorages all to ourselves, it will be sweet indeed to share a perfect anchorage with some of our new friends and to pass along its location to those who follow.

54° 50′ S, 68° 14′ W

Beagle Channel
Approaching Ushuaia, Argentina

December 26, 2001

. . . THREE one-thousand, four one-thousand, five one-thousand. There's the flash—five seconds," I call down to Evans.

"That's it—Islotes Eclaireurs," he says as he climbs up the companionway. The light a few miles ahead of us lies on the last of a chain of rocks and islands stretching almost across the five-mile-wide Beagle Channel. Leaving that light to port will give us a clear run behind those islands and into the harbor at Ushuaia, Argentina, the southernmost city in the world, less than seventy-five miles north of Cape Horn.

Six hours ago, in a mixture of sleet and rain under lowering clouds and in the company of dozens of Peale's dolphins, we rounded Cabo San Pio, on the south shore of Tierra del Fuego, and entered the sheltered waters of the Beagle Channel. Since then we have been navigating from buoy to buoy through the short high-latitude summer night, seeing little beyond the rounded silhouettes of rocky islets as they slipped past us in the poor visibility. The rain has now stopped and the clouds have lifted, but in the predawn light we can see little of the land around us. Evans climbs onto the port cockpit seat and looks over the hard dodger at the dazzle of city lights, twinkling and sparkling in the clear air, and their mirror image in the still black water of the channel. I climb onto the seat behind him and snuggle into his lee, seeking his warmth in the crisp forty-degree air. Slipping my arms around him I say, "So, you got what you wanted."

"Motoring up the Beagle in a flat calm," he says. "I can hardly believe it."

Since leaving Mar del Plata a month before, we have sailed some 1,500 miles south and west down the challenging Argentinean coast chased by near gale-force northwest winds on the falling barometer, seeking shelter in the few harbors along the route when the barometer leveled off, then sitting out twelve to thirty-six hours of gale- to storm-force southwesterlies while the barometer rocketed skyward. We measured weather windows in hours rather than days, and four fronts often passed over us in forty-eight hours. We haven't even raised the mainsail in the last two weeks, relying instead on our storm trysail and small jibs. When Evans told me he wanted to motor in light air rather than beating into thirty knots due west up the Beagle Channel on the last leg, we had both laughed.

Over the next hour, dawn creeps down the sides of the mountains and up the channel behind us, slowly revealing a rugged landscape of rocky mountains, rugged islets, and blue water. Snow-capped peaks line either side of the five-mile-wide channel, rising to 3,000 feet and more, their bases forested with a twisted mix of beech trees, their tops blasted to polished granite by tempestuous Cape Horn storms. Ushuaia, a colorful city of small, brightly-painted buildings, nestles under the high peaks and spills onto a low spit of land to the west. Beyond that spit, the Cordilla Darwin, a snowy mountain range studded with glaciers, recedes into the distance. The tallest peak, shining so brightly in the rising sun that it makes me blink, has to be Cerro Darwin itself, some 8,000 feet high.

All at once it hits me. We've made it. We are in the Beagle Channel. Getting here has so completely occupied me for the last several weeks that the sudden realization of being here takes me by surprise. When we drop anchor, our four-month, 8,000-nautical-mile run south from Iceland will be complete. From here, we will switch from passage mode to coastal cruising. Our course will turn west and north as we explore the labyrinth of canals, sounds, straits, and islands that make up the thousand-mile-long archipelago along Chile's west coast.

This is an ending of sorts, and I find myself trying to trace the thread that led to this moment, to identify the beginning, the instigating event that resulted in our being here now. "So how did all this start?" I ask Evans. "When did it begin?"

Evans is quiet for several minutes, and my own thoughts move backward in time, back to the Iceland, Ireland, and Newfoundland trips designed to build the skills we would need to sail down here, back to the investment of $400 in the Chilean chart kit before we even moved aboard, back to the hours invested in *Hawk*'s interior to keep it warm and dry in freezing temperatures, back to our design specifications for a hard dodger and a boat that could sail into thirty-knot winds and the accompanying seas, back to the decision to go with a metal boat and the implication that our voyaging would be in the higher latitudes. There could be no question that when we specified our next boat—indeed, when we made the fateful decision to go sailing again within a few months after returning aboard *Silk*—we had already decided not just on high-latitude sailing but more specifically on the Chilean channels.

"I think it first started with Ellard's *South American Pilot*," Evans says. Then I remember.

Seven—almost eight—years ago, we were on Rodrigues Island with our friends Clive and Laila from *Isa Lei*, their 30-foot fiberglass sloop, after the boisterous run across the Southern Indian Ocean. On that tiny speck of land six hundred miles or so to the west of Madagascar, we met Ellard and his five crew members aboard *Nicola*, a Roberts-designed steel cutter that Ellard built himself with dreams of rounding Cape Horn. But after thirty-four days in Southern Ocean gales and storms between Cape Town and Rodrigues, he had completely abandoned any thoughts of the Horn. He was, however, amused by our fears of rounding the Cape of Good Hope. "Let me show you a *real* Great Cape," he said, and gave his copy of the *South American Pilot* for Cape Horn and the Chilean channels to Evans and Clive. This began a running joke about the four of us sailing around the Horn after we put this "little cape" behind us.

Evans is right. What started as a ploy to ease the tension over rounding the Cape of Good Hope eventually led to this moment in the Beagle Channel. As our anchor splashes into the water off the city that calls itself "El Fin del Mundo" (the End of the Earth), the getting here ends. But the being here has just begun.

54° 52' S, 67° 21' W

Beagle Channel, Bahia Relegada
Tierra del Fuego, Argentina

January 27, 2002

GREAT grebe!" my sister, Leigh, exclaims as the anchor falls from *Hawk*'s bow at Bahia Relegada, on the southern shore of Argentinean Tierra del Fuego. Around the shore of the slotlike arm of the anchorage, scrubby bushes and spidery saplings invade long-ungrazed pastures. Beyond them, shiny-leaved beech trees roll up low hills fronting majestic snow-covered mountains some six to eight miles to the north. I look to where she is pointing and see a long-necked bird that I would have taken for a cormorant floating just at the surface of the water. She hands me the binoculars, and the fire red color on the neck and tail jump into focus along with the strangely upswept bill and raised black comb. "Breeding plumage," she tells me.

Leigh has spent the last week with us aboard *Hawk* exploring some of the anchorages along the Argentinean side of the Beagle Channel. Sailing has not been the major focus of this visit, as it had been when she and her husband joined us in the Caribbean on two earlier occasions. Instead our goal has been to observe some of the 120 species of indigenous birds.

Leigh has always been passionate about wildlife. While growing up we collected, observed, and released a plethora of reptiles and amphibians and temporarily adopted everything from chipmunks to—for one eventful summer—a raccoon. Leigh's love of birding began in those years, but as an environmental consultant she rarely has the time or opportunity to indulge it. Patagonia offered her a once in a lifetime chance to see some of the most interesting and least accessible bird species on the planet.

We picked up Leigh in Ushuaia a week ago and, after a lay day while Patagonia introduced itself with 40-knot winds, we headed east down the Beagle Channel. Within twenty minutes of leaving Ushuaia, Leigh was seeing "life birds"—species she had never seen before. Rafts of Magellanic penguins floated around the boat, many year-old juveniles wearing fuzzy gray suits. Black-browed albatrosses soared and dipped on their six-foot-long wings until the wind died away, leaving hundreds of birds scattered across the channel, becalmed. Tuxedoed black-and-white king cormorants floated low on the water, only their snakelike necks and pointed beaks visible. A half dozen other species flapped or floated by, to be captured in Leigh's binoculars.

But she wasn't satisfied merely to identify a bird, check it off the list, and move on. She wanted to know something of its life and habits, and I found myself digging along with her through the four guidebooks we had on board, trying to answer her questions. I was surprised to realize I had accumulated a good deal of knowledge, gleaned from five years of passive observation of the birds that accompanied us—sometimes for days—at sea.

Arctic terns, small swallowlike seabirds, complete an epic 16,000-mile journey every year, starting at their breeding grounds in Iceland in July and taking them to their wintering grounds in southern South America before returning north in March or April. The Magellanic diving petrel, small enough to fit easily in the palm of my hand, is equally comfortable flying through air or water, and often flies right through a wave in a storm at sea without a pause. Magellanic penguins, so awkward and comical on shore, turn into graceful acrobats in the water, where they live continuously from April to August, migrating up to 2,500 miles and as far north as the latitude of Rio de Janeiro, Brazil.

But my knowledge of birds ends at the breakers, and I have never attempted to sort out those that make their home along or onshore. Leigh led and I followed while we identified dozens of species. We watched flightless steamer ducks, goose-size birds that flee from danger using their wings as paddlewheels, propel themselves along like windup toys at up to thirty miles an hour. We heard the harsh, metallic honking of black-faced ibises before seeing them flying over in V formation, their beige and black flamingo-like bodies ending in foot-long downward-curved bills. Near the freshwater pool of a beaver dam, a pair of austral parakeets, the size of parrots with a dark green body and bright red tail, landed in a tree and acted every bit as startled to see us as we were to see them.

In the week we have been together, Leigh has opened my eyes to a world that has always been there but remained unseen until I chose to look. She has taught me that although many of the more common species in an area can be easily mastered, the moment of lifting the binoculars to confirm is one of endless possibility, where a brand-new, breathtakingly beautiful bird might be revealed masquerading as a well-known friend. With a small investment in awareness, this world opens itself, for it is neither shy nor hidden but—all too often—ignored.

With the anchor down, we are covering the mainsail so we can head below to the warmth of the diesel heater. But as I reach up to secure the end of the mainsail cover, I glimpse a large bird wheeling across the sky. "Leigh, look!"

Leigh has her binoculars up in an instant, and I hear a gasp. "Andean condor!"

I grab the second pair of binoculars, and a huge black bird comes into focus, its long wings stretched to catch the thermals, an "ermine" collar visible around its neck, and wide white windows flashing on the tops of the wings. The largest terrestrial bird of prey in the world, with a wingspan of more than ten feet, the Andean condor breeds at altitudes of 10,000 feet and can fly to more than 26,000 feet. Many birders wait a lifetime to see such a bird. From *Hawk's* decks, all I have to do is raise my head.

54° 56′ S, 67° 37′ W

m/v *Micalvi*, Club de Yates
Puerto Williams, Chile

February 8, 2002

So, did you find what you were looking for?" I ask. I study the man sitting next to me, a man I first met a little less than a month ago in Ushuaia, Argentina. Craig was waiting for the charter boat that would take him to Antarctica, and when we invited him aboard *Hawk*, he arrived, clean-shaven and fresh-scrubbed, with a bottle of wine. Around forty years old with sandy hair mixed with gray, the compact and muscular body of a serious hiker and the inquisitive mind of an inveterate traveler, Craig told us then that he wanted to see a bit of nature untouched by man before it was too late.

Now *Hawk* and the *Alaska Eagle*, the yacht that Craig crewed to Antarctica and back, lie tied alongside the *Micalvi* in Puerto Williams, Chile, and Craig and I sit talking amongst the murmuring conversations, flag- and photo-bedecked walls, and wood-fire warmth of the southernmost—and funkiest—yacht club in the world. The ex-*Micalvi*, a 200-foot-long, half-sunken, onetime ammunitions carrier, lies in an almost perfectly protected inlet to the west of the Chilean naval base, on the mountainous and rugged Isla Navarino, just sixty miles north of Cape Horn. Boats stop here before and after completing the week or so of daysails that take them around the Horn, and before and after the 600-mile run across Drake Passage to Antarctica.

Their crews cross the steel walkway spanning the flooded bilges at the vessel's beam and pass through the watertight gray door into the bar, with its mahogany wainscoting and low ceilings. Pitchers of the Chilean national drink, Pisco sours, made from fermented white wine and lemons, help fortify them to face the difficulties of an upcoming voyage or release the tension from one just completed. I watched Craig's crew file in earlier this evening, just a few hours after returning from their three-week round-trip to Antarctica. No sense of celebration or accomplishment accompanied them through the door. Rather they all exuded an abstracted, shell-shocked air, as if some vital part of them still lay mired in the icy, barren wilderness to the south of us.

Fight and flight are not the only reactions to life-threatening situations. Freeze has proven a time-honored survival mechanism for many species, humans included.

When Craig came and sat down next to me, I noticed a week's worth of white and gray bristles covering his chin and cheeks, and dark hollows under his eyes. I have plenty of time to study his face before he answers my question. "Well," he says, "it certainly was untouched." But I can tell he no longer thinks that's the point. He lapses into silence, and I see him struggling to find words to convey what he experienced.

The other people we met coming back from Antarctica struggled in exactly the same way. With close to 100,000 miles of offshore sailing behind them, our Dutch friends Aad and Hella, on the 48-foot steel ketch *Helena Cristina*, would only say, "You just have to go and see it for yourselves." The crew of three who accompanied them clearly felt that Antarctica was too large, too alien, to be encompassed by mere words. They wore the same weary survivor expression I see on Craig's face. I recognize that expression; I know it has been on my face a few times in my life—times when I came up against my limits and had to push through them or give in to them.

One of Aad's crew gave in. An experienced sailor seasoned by North Sea gales, he said he became terrified—not of anything specific but of the idea of the Drake Passage, the Horn, Antarctica. He crawled into his bunk and couldn't be threatened or cajoled back out of it. Such stories are far from uncommon. Tina and Gustaf, on *Caminante*, and Becky and Evans, on *Finnrose*, took on crew in Mar del Plata, Argentina, for the trip south to the Beagle Channel. Both couples had to put their crews ashore a few hundred miles south at the first good harbor after being hove-to in 50 knots for twenty-four hours. We heard of similar situations aboard many of the charter boats that went to Antarctica. Fight and flight are not the only reactions to life-threatening situations. Freeze has proven a time-honored survival mechanism for many species, humans included.

We have been pushed to our limits on only two passages, and in both cases the worse it got, the harder Evans fought. But the worse it got, the more I wanted to climb into my bunk, close my eyes, and wish it all away. Forcing myself out of the (relative) security and comfort of my bunk, into my foul-weather gear and out into the cockpit, remains the hardest thing I have ever done. Both of us pushed through what we had thought were our absolute limits. After a passage like that, we don't make landfall and celebrate. It takes weeks and sometimes months to recuperate, to integrate what we learned about ourselves, good and bad, into our self-image and our worldview.

So I understand the haunted, abstracted expression on Craig's face. As I look around at the group of people still wound tight despite the ministrations of the bartender and his Pisco sours, I know that although their eyes may have registered an icy, frigid landscape, reflected within that barren, windswept world they saw the best and worst of who they were. From the dazed look on their faces, many are not yet sure how they feel about that.

When Craig speaks again, it isn't about Antarctica. "I was at the helm when we made landfall at Cape Horn at dawn," he says slowly. "We were bashing through the waves into forty knots of wind under the triple-reefed main and the number four jib." He goes on to describe the stony island rising up out of the sea, the feel of the wind and the pull of the helm, the sun shining silver on the water. His words are articulate and expressive. He can not tell me about Antarctica, but he can tell me about this.

Craig found what he was looking for, and it wasn't unspoiled wilderness. He is surer of who he is and what he wants than when we met him three weeks ago. The voyage has changed him. I wonder if he has yet begun to realize how much.

54° 56′ S, 69° 09′ W

Caleta Olla
Northwest arm of the Beagle Channel
Tierra del Fuego, Chile

February 10, 2002

Picture a thousand miles of virtually uninhabited coastline with mountains rising several thousand feet straight out of the sea and glaciers calving into the water at their bases; a place almost completely untouched by man except for a few small fishing villages tucked at the end of long fjords that run for miles straight into the Andes range. For three years, while we were building *Hawk*, that's how I answered the dozens of people who asked why we wanted to cruise the Chilean channels. Most people would pause at my response. Perhaps, for a few seconds, they glimpsed the vision that drove Evans and me. But I could see the moment when they recalled the many disadvantages of cruising the high latitudes.

Intellectually, we knew that cruising above 50 degrees latitude would be occasionally uncomfortable, often stressful, and always challenging. Parts of Chile's west coast experience more than 300 days of precipitation per year. Snow and freezing temperatures occur at the height of the southern summer. The pilot charts for the area show average winds of 25 knots with winds in excess of 35 knots one day in five or six—comparable to Ireland in the middle of winter. Katabatic winds blast downward off the snow-capped rocky mountains in *racha*s, or williwaws, capable of knocking down a fifty-foot yacht. Yet somehow the vivid and compelling vision of glaciers calving into the sea obscured the equally real possibility of *Hawk* being slammed flat by a hurricane-force williwaw.

As with all of the cruising we have done, the reality exceeds the best and worst we were capable of imagining. The Chilean navy doesn't waste *avisos de malo tiempo*—advisories of bad weather—on gale-force winds; they typically herald fifty knots with gusts to seventy. Hand steering in the squally and gusty southwest winds on a rising barometer requires neoprene gloves and balaclava to protect hands and face from the stinging hail capable of raising welts on bare flesh. Three days out of four we can see little through the driving rain or pelting hail except the bases of the high mountains that border the channels.

Of the six boats that came down the Argentinean coast at the same time we did, one was dismasted in the Straits of Le Maire after having made it around the Horn; one was twice knocked down past the horizontal in 70-knot winds while offshore near Puerto Montt; one dragged anchor in 60 knots and almost went up on the rocks at Picton Island, in the eastern entrance to the Beagle Channel; and another hit the rocks when caught by *racha*s while trying to maneuver into a sheltered cove on Staten Island. Yet none but the dismasted boat suffered damage so severe that it could not continue.

There's that reality—and another. In the last few months, we have barely scratched the surface of the Chilean channels: a thousand miles of the Scottish isles at three times the scale; the islets and channels of Maine set against the mountains of Yosemite; a place without towns or marinas let alone lobster pots or tourists. As best as we can tell, about two dozen cruising boats have been wandering around in tens of thousands of square miles of islands and channels, about a quarter of it uncharted. In a typical week, dolphins guide us into and out of our anchorage, sea lions play with us when we explore by

dinghy, and a dozen species of seabirds feed in frantic flocks over seething shoals of fish. We may well be seeing the last habitable area on Earth that has yet to be shaped by man's hand, and turned to his purposes.

A couple of the boats that came down the Argentinean coast with us left the channels hundreds of miles earlier than intended, their crews eager to exchange gale-force headwinds and three layers of clothes for trade winds over the stern and no clothes at all.

But . . . picture the northwest arm of the Beagle Channel, a thirty-mile stretch of water averaging two miles or so in width, bordered by sheer mountains rising to 4,000 to 8,000 feet. Picture a half dozen major glaciers rolling in rivers of white ice down from the peaks to reach sea level in the channel itself. Picture the wide horizontal fractures in that river of ice and the colors that flash from the compressed walls within these striations—the breathtaking blue of sapphire and the hard green glow of emerald.

Picture sailing in the milky water, turned from sea green to chalky lime by the sediment from a millennia of grinding pressure where ice meets rock. Picture entering Caleta Olla, the easternmost anchorage in the Beagle's northwest arm. Lacy clouds spread delicate tendrils across the cutoff face of the cleaved peak, rising 6,000 feet above white snowfields, while the low-angled rays of the sun reveal a range of orange and red highlights within the sheer face of gray rock. The pristine snow covers the steep slopes below the peak, running down for several thousand feet to the altitude where the Nothofagus beech forest begins. The broad band of trees ends at a sheer cliff hundreds of feet high at the head of the harbor that we are entering.

The snowfield turns to glacier ice just above the trees, and sweeps down around the edge of the forest. The broad curve of white snow and blue ice has cut its way down a ravine, rising to a height well above tree level, leaving broken trunks along its edge that look no larger than matchsticks. One final twist at the bottom of the ravine, and the glacier ice spills around the edge of the cliff and expires at sea level, a mile or two from the shore of the bay we are entering.

Can you picture it? Would it be worth the williwaws? Many sailors, maybe most, would say no. But standing here on *Hawk*'s deck surrounded by the milky green water of the glacier melt, with that sheer cliff towering above me, I can tell you that it is worth it for Evans and for me.

49° 07′ S, 74° 25′ W

Paso del Indio
Puerto Eden, Chile

March 5, 2002

NINE of us sit crowded around the main saloon table aboard the 43-foot steel ketch *Caminante* while first-mate Tina ransacks the galley in search of more glasses. Evans Hoyt, from the Fiskar 45 *Finnrose*, pops the cork on the champagne as his partner, Becky, lines up the glasses to be filled. Ishiro, a Japanese single-hander aboard a Midget 26 called *Aurora*, stacks the cake dishes and coffee cups from the first round of our celebration. After several minutes of closely confined chaos, a ragged assortment of plastic glasses is raised into the air. We all look at one another until Gustaf, *Caminante*'s skipper, says, "Fifty to fifty."

In the pause that follows those words, I find myself hesitating. Fifty to fifty. Gustaf's toast refers to the clipper ship definition of rounding the Horn—sailing nonstop south from

50° S around the tucked-under tail of South America and back north to 50° S. Yesterday Evans and I crossed the magic 50-degree line on our northbound voyage and reached Puerto Eden, the halfway point on a journey up the thousand miles of channels along Chile's west coast and the only settlement we have seen since leaving the Beagle Channel. But we certainly haven't done it nonstop, and we elected not to sail around the Horn though we were within sixty miles of it. After our 8,000-nautical mile voyage down the length of the Atlantic, sailing an additional sixty miles to round a battered headland, no matter how infamous, had seemed an anticlimax. Somehow it has become a point of honor for us and several of the crews here with us *not to* go to Cape Horn. We aren't Cape Horners.

We reached Puerto Eden yesterday after an exhilarating eighty-mile daysail. It started when we left our anchorage to follow a ribbon of water shining like quicksilver under the three-quarter moon that led out from our anchorage and between the dark bulk of a dozen islands. A few hours later, the long, slanting rays of the rising sun transformed the bushy blows of humpback whales into a shower of gold against the gray loom of cloud and mountain. By midday we were sailing past decaying icebergs that had calved from Pio XI—one of the largest glaciers in the world—some fifty miles inland. Bright sunshine alternated with hail and 40-knot winds in fast-moving squalls that left a scattering of rainbows in their wakes.

A perfect day became something more, something to celebrate, when we arrived to find the friends we first met in Mar del Plata four months ago and last saw at a New Year's Eve party in Ushuaia in the Beagle Channel. The greetings from the crews aboard the yachts tied to the wharf brought big smiles to both our faces. Two Swedes, Pål and Maria, joined Tina and Gustaf aboard *Caminante* in Ushuaia and would be getting off the boat in Puerto Eden to catch a ferry for the rest of the voyage up the channels. Becky and Evans Hoyt, on *Finnrose*, were giving a lift to a young Chilean fisherman named Alex for the

200-mile trip to his home near Tortel, a small settlement lying at the foot of the Andes in a basin between the northern and southern Patagonian ice caps. Ishiro sailed the channels alone in his 26-foot boat except for his cat, Fuente, and planned to head offshore sixty miles north at the Golfo de Penas. After sharing only two anchorages and seeing only four other people in the last six weeks, we were ready for some socializing.

But refueling and reprovisioning came first. Four yachts and ten crew members took the tiny fishing settlement of four hundred by storm. We wandered along the wooden boardwalks that meandered over the steep, uneven terrain and the dense, bushy vegetation, past the stilt-legged houses. We raided the half dozen one-room shops for eggs, potatoes, onions, and anything else that wasn't dust-covered. Manuel, the owner of the hardware store, and his assistant rolled fifty-five-gallon drums of diesel along the boardwalks, levered them up the steps and over the bumps, then sent them clattering down the last three steps and out onto the wharf where three of the yachts lay rafted. Alex introduced us to his friends and relatives, one of whom produced a fish for Ishiro to feed to his cat. A gnarled brown-skinned woman with eyes like raisins and a toothless smile sold me the last round loaf of dense white bread, warm and smoky from the open hearth where it had been baked.

When every tank and jerry jug had been filled and we had given up on finding anything else edible, we all descended on *Caminante* to enjoy the cake we had smelled for much of the afternoon. As we sipped coffee and caught up on one another's adventures while south of 50 degrees, the conversation moved from Spanish to Swedish to English and back with frequent pauses for translation. "*El agua es blanco como leche,*" explained Alex, trying to describe the milky glacier meltwater near his home. "We sailed white up Estero Pitt," Becky said, referring to sailing through one of the many channels shown only as white space without soundings on the Chilean charts.

Now, with the cake disposed of and the first round of celebration behind us, my eyes meet those of the others around the table over our raised glasses. I think of all the shared experiences behind the few words, of the e-mails and SSB conversations advising about safe anchorages and bad weather, about the bond forged in Mar del Plata and strengthened over four months. None of us is a Cape Horner. Evans and I are cruising sailors who have pushed ourselves every step of the way, who have felt stress and frustration and fear when confronted by the area's tempestuous weather and who have not always dealt gracefully with each other in this harsh environment. But we have been south of 50° S with others who know what that means. I raise my glass a bit higher and in unison with the rest toast our own version of fifty to fifty.

44° 28′ S, 73° 38′ W

Isla Filomena
Canal Moraleda, Chile

March 18, 2002

EVANS licks the last of the chocolate cake batter from the serving spoon and puts the spoon back into the bowl. "When was the last time we lazed on deck in T-shirts?" he asks.

I drop down next to where he is sitting on the coach roof, lie back, and close my eyes, luxuriating in the feel of the warm sun kissing my face and caressing my bare arms. My mind searches back over 3,000 miles and five months, to northern Argentina and our final days in the tropics, before I come up with a memory of voluntarily spending time above decks in anything less than three layers of clothes. "Mar del Plata," I murmur. I roll over and look at him. "I can hardly believe that less than two hundred miles south of here you were wearing your survival suit while we sailed through the brash ice fronting a glacier face."

Since crossing the Golfo de Penas at 47° S three days ago, we have entered a whole different world. Golfo de Penas, or Gulf of Pain, represents a major milestone for those cruising Chile's archipelago—the only place where yachts must leave the shelter of the channels to brave the Roaring Forties on a dangerous and shoal lee shore. But it also represents a major transition in climate and geography.

When we sailed out Canal Messier and entered the Golfo de Penas, we left behind the tortured, bonsai-like trees clinging to the bases of rain-scoured, wind-ravaged mountains and the katabatic winds blasting across anchorages and raising mini-waterspouts. We entered Bahia Anna Pink, just north of 46° S, to find lower, rounder islands, their silhouettes softened by forests of tall, straight beech and conifers that afford real protection from stronger winds. In the last few days, we have sailed past the occasional field or grassy area and working and abandoned fishing camps—a surprise after the many months spent in a raw, brutal, virtually uninhabited land. The barometer rocketed above 1012 millibars for the first time in several months, and sunshine and warm weather have replaced the torrential rain two days out of three and the gale- to storm-force winds once or twice a week that we grew used to farther south. The wind, which blew anywhere from 30 degrees apparent forward for all but two days out of two months south of the Golfo de Penas, shifted aft when we came into Bahia Anna Pink. Instead of motor sailing, we have been able to sail every one of the last three days. It's as if, in a 120-mile overnight passage, we left the Chilean channels far behind and were somehow transported to the gentle landscapes and temperate weather of southern Ireland or Nova Scotia.

"You know what I like?" Evans asks as he stretches out on the deck beside me. "Just dropping an anchor and not taking an hour and a half to put shore lines out. I never appreciated how simple and easy that was before this."

"I like swinging to the wind and not having rain coming in over the stern," I tell him. "I like being able to sail again."

"You know, within a few days we'll be back in civilization. After almost two months we'll be in a place with telephones, supermarkets, Laundromats, Internet cafes, restaurants, bakeries . . ."

"Post offices. Postcards. People."

The soft breeze rustles the green branches overhead. Evans looks at me. "No wonder so many crews never take their boats south of the Golfo de Penas."

"It's nice to be warm again, isn't it? Nice not to be worried about the weather. Nice to go exploring in the dinghy and walking ashore."

We lie there, feeling *Hawk*'s gentle motions as she moves to the breeze, watching a hawklike brown bird watching us from a treetop. The warmth on my face and the perfect floating feeling have almost lulled me to sleep when Evans says, "We don't have to go south again next spring if you don't want to."

That has been the plan all along. Make our way from the bottom of South America north up the channels, against the prevailing wind, to Puerto Montt, where the Chilean archipelago ends. Winter in Puerto Montt, then back south again, with the wind, back to the Beagle Channel. Now Evans is suggesting—what? Head into the Pacific? I try the idea on for size, let my mind absorb it, play with it. "You mean give up cold weather, thermal underwear, storms, and shore lines for tropical waters, sunshine, warmth, and trade winds?"

Evans's eyes meet mine. "Maybe."

The blows of humpback whales backed by misty mountains. The freight train rumble of the wind two minutes before it

reaches the boat. The cobalt blue of a glacier face shattered by a ray of sunshine into a dozen hues between teal and purple. The paralyzing sight of a williwaw hitting the water like a fist, sending up a perfect circle of white spume fifty feet across. The greetings of shy fishermen isolated for months at a time in their fishing camps. The clenched-stomach sensation when Evans releases the last shore line and *Hawk* swings toward a rock as I desperately try to clear the chain of kelp. The breathtaking beauty of 5,000-foot-high snow-capped peaks rising straight from the sea on either side of a mile-wide channel. Image after image cascades through my mind, vivid and intense.

I sigh. "Maybe not."

Evans smiles.

41° 30' S, 72° 58' W

Marina del Sur
Puerto Montt, Chile

September 11, 2002

ONE year ago, Evans and I were in the Canaries preparing *Hawk* for the 800-mile passage to the Cape Verde islands. While I made the sea bunks and Evans deflated the dinghy, a BBC program droned away on the shortwave radio. I can't remember what program it was, but even now, writing this, I can feel a ghost of the "this can't be happening" sensation that clenched my stomach at the announcement of a plane crashing into one of the twin towers of the World Trade Center. We did not leave the Canaries that day. And when we did get under way on September 12, we knew we left more than the islands in our wake, though we could not articulate exactly what we had lost.

We arrived in the Cape Verdes islands, located less than 400 miles off the coast of Senegal, a week later. The islands gained their independence from Portugal only in 1975, and though considered safe and stable by African standards, the country numbers among the poorest in the world. The economy runs on a combination of international aid and money from relatives who have been fortunate enough to find work—legally or otherwise—in Europe or the United States.

At Porto Grande, on Isla de São Vicente, faded colonial buildings lined rutted cobblestone streets where flies buzzed around piles of rags, garbage, and dog excrement. Gaunt mahogany-colored men squatted with their backs braced against the rough stone walls of the buildings, talking, smoking, and spitting. Well-padded ebony women wearing multicolored dresses sat behind piles of dusty vegetables and fruits and swung their hands in a languid gesture every few minutes to ward off the flies. In the half dozen stores, a chaos of goods slid off canted shelves onto wood-planked floors, almost blocking the narrow, dimly lit aisles. Dried fruit and root vegetables and colorful beans jostled against plastic laundry tubs and alcohol stoves; bottles of imported mineral water stood stacked in waist-high rows, their carefully camouflaged broken seals indicating that many had been refilled with the suspect local water. None of these stores sold meat of any kind, nor did they offer any refrigerated or frozen items. For dairy products we had our choice of Velveeta cheese, canned butter, UHT milk, and large bags of dried milk labeled as United Nations food aid, "Not for resale."

And then there was the Shell station.

The modern, sleek gasoline pumps, wiped of dust regularly by one of the uniformed attendants, stood a hundred feet off the beach, equally well positioned to serve automobiles or boats. Across the street, no men leaned against the white-scrubbed facade of the "mini-mart," and no one spit on the perfectly swept sidewalk in front of it. The arctic blast of the air-conditioning raised goose bumps on my skin as we entered the store, where neatly packaged goods lined rows of shoulder-height shelves spaced wide enough for nonexistent shopping carts. Perfectly aligned boxes of cornflakes and Fruit Loops stood at attention opposite brightly colored bags of Lay's potato chips and Fritos, each package costing twice what it would in the United States and the equivalent of two days' wages in the Cape Verdes. Along the back wall, old-fashioned glass bottles labeled Coke and Sprite and Pepsi peeked through the doors of refrigerated cases, their curved outlines blurred by the cold sweat of condensation. In one corner, a cappuccino machine and a microwave flanked a cluster of stand-up tables. Here, pretty young ladies wearing miniskirted uniforms popped the caps off the cold drinks we had selected, then watched anxiously to be sure we didn't leave without returning the bottles.

Even ten days earlier, the utter incongruity of that store on that street in those islands might have made a fleeting impression, or it might have escaped my notice completely. But with rescue workers still searching the twisted wreckage of the World Trade Center for survivors, I saw how this store's presence created a division where none had existed before, forcing comparison and inviting judgment. It intruded itself into the chaotic swirl of color and life on the street without in any way acknowledging it or taking part in it. And it made me feel an uneasy sense of disquiet—something I had felt before.

During our six months wintering in Ireland, we talked to many people who blamed the failure of the Easter Sunday peace agreement on well-meaning Irish Americans who, they claimed, continued to provide the money that fueled the bloody struggle between the two tiny factions holding Britain and Ireland hostage. In Iceland a few months later, we witnessed firsthand the anti-U.S. sentiments that have erupted as violent protests over the country's increasing economic reliance on payments for the American base in Reykjavik. Here in Chile, people talk openly and unemotionally about how the Central Intelligence Agency (CIA) in conjunction with a group of American corporations, including the now-defunct ITT, overthrew popularly elected reformist President Allende in 1973 and launched General Pinochet's military dictatorship.

Whether or not these things are true does not matter in the slightest—just as it makes no difference that Royal Dutch Shell is not an American company. These perceptions inform people's beliefs and attitudes and illustrate the almost unimaginable reach, power, and influence that the United States has throughout the world. I can think of hardly anything that Ireland, Iceland, Chile, or the Cape Verdes could do that would intrude on the daily lives of Americans, yet the symbols of American power intrude into the lives of each of these country's citizens on a daily basis.

September 11 forced me to acknowledge this fundamental asymmetry, the gradual awareness of which has come from living on a small boat in foreign lands with one foot on each side of the global divide. When we left the Canaries, I left behind not innocence but willful ignorance. I have been unable to view the world, or America's place in it, in the same way since.

Caleta Anahuac
Puerto Montt, Chile

October 5, 2002

THE ancient bus wheezes and groans, the gears grind, and with a jerk it begins to move forward as I hand the driver our 400 pesos and follow Evans to an empty brown Naugahyde seat. The big, dark eyes of the younger *chilenos* follow our progress, and I smile at one little girl with a round olive face under straight black hair. She is sitting stiffly in her mother's lap, and she ducks her head away from me and blushes. Ours are the only brightly colored clothes, light hair, and white skins in sight, and we are the tallest people on the bus. Almost all *chilenos* are descended from the blending of the native Indian tribes with their Spanish conquerors, resulting in bronze complexions, thick black hair, and an average height several inches below my five foot four.

The bus gathered way and I look out over the corrugated tin roofs and plastic-covered windows of the stilt-legged wooden houses in the little fishing community of Anahuac. In the channel beyond, I can see dozens of small and large fishing boats lying at anchor and on buoys, their bows pointing into the gusting wind that traces white-laced patterns across the dark water. A cluster of masts stands tall at a bend in the channel about two miles away at Marina del Sur, where *Hawk*, fully stowed and provisioned for a spring passage south down the Chilean channels, still lies in her winter berth. We are stuck in harbor, as are the rafts of fishing boats. The port is closed to any vessels under twenty-five tons due to the atrocious weather, and it has been closed for the past three days, ever since we got our *zarpe* (cruising permit) and were cleared to leave.

We listened to the Patagonian Cruiser's Net on the SSB this morning and heard our friends who left two weeks ago describing conditions. "We had sixty knots in here last night and it's still blowing fifty," said Ken, aboard the Defever 40 trawler *Pelagic.* "*Discovery* is less than a hundred feet from us and we can't see her for the spray." The two boats have been sitting for eight days about 150 miles south of us, held by six anchors and ten lines in a barely tenable anchorage they just managed to reach when the bad weather moved in

It seems I cast off the twin restraints of comfort and trepidation with the docklines. I suddenly realize how ready I am to leave, how necessary it is for me to get back to our exciting and challenging life.

unexpectedly. Listening made real all the challenges and risks we would face when we left the safety and security of the marina and returned to our nomadic existence, our well-being totally dependent upon the strength of our vessel and our own ingenuity. A traitorous part of me whispers how lucky we are that the port is closed and hopes it might not reopen anytime soon.

The bus creeps up the final hill that will bring us into the town of Puerto Montt, the driver downshifting until the bus is in first gear and moving at no more than walking pace. Just before the crest, a small white church overlooks the channel below, and most of the people around us make the sign of the cross, then kiss their loose fists. Above the bus driver, several rosaries swing to the palsied movements of the straining vehicle. These are surrounded by pictures of the Virgin and a single curvaceous silhouette with measurements as improbable as a Barbie doll's. After months riding these buses along this route, I have almost stopped noticing these little details, but now I savor each with the heightened clarity of leave-taking.

Puerto Montt's unique mix of First and Third World charmed us on our first ride into town: the horse-drawn carts jockeying for position among the buses and trucks, or left "parked" at the curb; the vendors selling fruits and vegetables or dried kelp and bottled mussels from wheelbarrows in the narrow street behind the U.S.-style supermarket; the half-wild dogs wandering in packs across the pedestrian walkway leading to the glass-front mall with its high-class stores. We are comfortable here now, know where to find the post office and the port captain, which supermarkets carry the best variety of foods, and which hardware stores have silicone sealant and duct tape. As cruisers, we rarely stay long enough in one spot to enjoy the easy familiarity we have achieved here in Puerto Montt, and I feel a pang of regret. Soon enough we will leave it behind, along with the many friends we have made on other yachts and ashore.

SEVERAL hours later, I stand on *Hawk*'s foredeck as she swings to her anchor off Anahuac, surrounded by the fishing boats I saw earlier from the bus. The wind has dropped away to nothing, and the forecast calls for mild weather tomorrow, so on our return from town we decided to get off the dock and make sure everything still functioned, including us.

For the first time in many months, *Hawk* adjusts herself to the movement of wind and water, animate again, seemingly sentient, eager to spread her wings and fly. Her restless motions send a mixture of anticipation and excitement surging through me. It seems I cast off the twin restraints of comfort and trepidation with the docklines. I suddenly realize how ready I am to leave, how necessary it is for me to get away from the routine in Puerto Montt and back to our exciting and challenging life. I take one last look at the familiar shore and the narrow channel, at the marina where we spent the winter and the office where I wrote tens of thousands of words, then head down below to pull out the sea boots and the foul-weather gear for an early-morning departure.

45° 28′ S, 74° 45′ W

Golfo de Penas, Chile

October 19, 2002

A BRIGHT half-moon weaves silver into the heaving seas as we leave the shelter of Canal Darwin. *Hawk* bucks and plunges as she meets the Southern Ocean swell made steep and almost square by its encounter with Chile's continental shelf. We can just make out the dark silhouettes of the off-lying islands in the moonlight. As we pass the last dangers some ten miles from the entrance to Canal Darwin and turn south toward the Golfo de Penas, the rising sun brings a flush of color to the distant snowfields of the Andes. The wind matches the previous evening's forecast—15 knots just forward of the beam—and *Hawk* is making a good seven knots along her course despite the large swell.

With the exception of the hundred-mile-long section centered around 47° S, Chile's fractured and fragmented coastline can be navigated without venturing into the inhospitable waters of the Roaring Forties. In most places, ten to fifteen miles of islands and channels separate cruising boats from the Southern Ocean swell, so most sailing down here is done in flat water even in the frequent gale-force winds. The passage across the open waters of the Golfo de Penas represents a physical barrier for the many small fishing boats and foreign yachts that cruise this coast and a mental barrier for their crews. We heard innumerable stories during our winter in Puerto Montt about boats that had come to grief in the shoal waters and fearsome waves of the Golfo de Penas, and the local sailors and fishermen all asked nervously how our crossing had been when we were coming north. *"Es muy peligroso"*—it's very dangerous—they would say, shaking their heads. The Admiralty South American Pilot, not given to overstatement or the sailor's need for embellishment, says simply, "Winds of great force and very heavy seas are experienced in the gulf."

Although the Golfo de Penas may be a uniquely challenging place on a difficult coast, we have discovered that every sailing ground has its point of no return, its "Here be dragons," where most small fishing boats and local sailboats turn back and only a few noncommercial vessels continue onward. In Scotland it was Ardnamurchan Point, the last point passed by yachts leaving protected waters to head out across the notorious Minch, the thirty-mile-wide stretch of water separating the Inner Hebrides from the Outer. Yachts venturing beyond Ardnamurchan Point return with a sprig of heather tied to their bow pulpit to signify the accomplishment.

Where I first started sailing, our Ardnamurchan was called Stony Point. My father bought his first sailboat, a 24-foot Bristol Corsair, while I was in college. He kept the *Canadian Mist* in Chaumont Bay, on the northeast corner of Lake Ontario, and I got my first taste of cruising in that large, sheltered sound and the protected waters of Henderson Harbor, just to the south. Stony Point marks the entrance to Henderson Harbor, and beyond that lies the open waters of the eastern end of Lake Ontario, where fast-moving summer thunderstorms can bring howling winds and nasty seas almost without warning. But those brave enough to venture past Stony Point and across the twenty-some miles of open water beyond it reach a rich cruising ground—the sheltered waters of the St. Lawrence Seaway, home to the Thousand Islands and the quaint Canadian cities of Kingston and Ganonoque.

The first time I tried that crossing, twenty years ago now, I was with my boyfriend (at that time) aboard my father's boat and we were turned back by a summer thunderstorm halfway across. I still remember retching over the side while trying to pull down the jib as the *Canadian Mist* bounced and crashed into the suddenly steep seas. Right then, I hated sailing.

The first time Evans and I sailed together, some five years after that aborted attempt and four years before we bought *Silk* and left on our circumnavigation, we took that same boat across that same stretch of water and to the Thousand Islands. I vividly recall staring into the rainbows dancing in the bow wave on that glorious day and trying to touch my future self to see what I would be doing in a decade or two. Sailing was not yet part of my life, and Evans would not begin trying to convince me to go cruising for another two years. I would never have believed that a circumnavigation lay in my future, along with Ardnamurchan Point and the Golfo de Penas.

Two hours after turning south toward the gulf, *Hawk* is pounding into 25 knots of apparent wind right up our course and a big, nasty sea that slows our progress to less than four knots every few minutes. The wind seems to be building, and the seas with it. Clearly the forecast was wrong. "What do you think?" Evans asks me.

"It's not worth it," I say. "We can't make the course. We're beating ourselves up for nothing." He nods his agreement, spins the wheel as I ease the mainsheet, and we fly back toward Canal Darwin at 9 knots. Two days later, we sail past the San Pedro lighthouse and enter Canal Messier after a fast and easy fifteen-hour crossing of the notorious gulf.

All seas have their dangers, their tide rips and freak waves and unpredictable winds and uncharted rocks. All waters require local knowledge, good judgment, and a great deal of respect. Every sailor out cruising started by equipping a capable boat and sailing past his or her Ardnamurchan Point. Some of them turned around the first time; most turned around at one time or another when they saw that conditions weren't right. But they weren't afraid to try again.

Cape Horn

December 14, 2002

I GRIP the handhold on the back of the hard dodger to brace myself against the large ocean swell. Ahead of us, past the blasted, eroded islands to port and starboard, lies a low, wedge-shaped green piece of land with two towering rock spires scraping at the clear blue sky. The huge swell breaks over anything less than ten meters in depth, rendering the locations of underwater rocks and shoals spectacularly clear. Some eight miles ahead of us, a mile or so off the canted island, geysers of whitewater shoot fifty feet into the air every few seconds. Even in ten-knot winds and bright sunshine, the sense of movement from the breaking water and the rolling swell make it seem as though the whole sea seethes and crashes and dashes itself ashore right here, on this lonely island at the bottom of a continent.

Impossible as it seemed, this first view of Isla Hornos—Horn Island—lives up to the myths and legends surrounding it.

Named for the Dutch town of Hoorn, which sponsored the voyage that discovered it in 1616, Cabo de Hornos—Cape Horn—lies at the southern end of the southernmost island in a battered archipelago called the Wollastons, some fifty miles southwest of the entrance to the Beagle Channel. Crews wanting to go to the Horn have to get a special cruising permit from the Armada, the Chilean navy. This *zarpe* allows yachts to anchor in a single anchorage in the Wollaston Islands, Caleta Martial, and specifies the exact route they must take in sailing around the Horn. The entire Wollaston archipelago is now a national park, and crews are required to remain in radio contact with the Armada throughout their visit. Chilean naval vessels patrol the area almost constantly, and immense cruise ships call at Cape Horn several times a week. All in all, it seemed to us that sailing to the Horn was no longer the adventure it used to be.

That was part of the reason why we hadn't chosen to make this voyage upon our arrival in the Beagle Channel a year ago. We had, in fact, decided to be one of the only crews—if not the only one—to spend two seasons in Chile without actually visiting the legendary headland. But on our return trip south down the channels, we kept being asked by well-meaning friends and relatives if we were going to do the Horn *again*. They all assumed we had already passed under Cape Horn when we had been in these waters the year before. By the time we reached Puerto Williams, we were tired of correcting everyone, and we felt as though we had no choice but to make the short voyage south to the Horn. As we motored away from the *Micalvi* yesterday, Evans said, "This is the first time we've ever done anything on either boat because others think we should, not because we want to."

Our blasé attitude didn't last more than a few hours. Cape Horn chose to remind us that the sea doesn't change, nor does the unpredictable weather that has destroyed so many vessels and made this headland infamous.

Last night the wind shifted when we were still in the shallow waters of Bahia Nassau, some twelve miles from our anchorage in the Wollastons. It did so almost instantaneously, swinging from northwest to southwest in the space of several fitful gusts, each stronger than the last. In less than a minute, we went from running to beating, from 12 knots of apparent wind to more than thirty. We spent the next six hours trying to beat our way into winds that increased to 40 knots, then 45, then 50. When we saw a steady 60 knots of apparent wind on our anemometer for the first time ever, Evans yelled, "Welcome to Cape Horn weather!"

This morning we woke to blue skies and calm winds, a startling contrast to last night's wild weather. As we approach

Cathedral Rocks, the twin spires off the northern corner of Isla Hornos, we can see waves breaking in huge plumes of white-water over the jagged teeth of the partially submerged boulders at their bases. The sea seethes in colors from cobalt blue to mint green under the maelstrom of spume. But the thrill I feel at the sight is tempered by sadness and worry. Just an hour ago, a Chilean navy ship rendezvoused with us in Caleta Martial.

Six members of her crew boarded *Hawk* in order to inspect our EPIRB (emergency position-indicating radio beacon). They told us they had received an emergency distress signal from the area of Cape Horn the previous night. After a thorough inspection of the boat and the switch on our still-sealed EPIRB, they wished us a good day and told us we could proceed to the Horn. *"Hace buen tiempo. Disfruten!"* (It's beautiful weather. Enjoy yourselves!) But I cannot enjoy myself knowing that another yacht may have gotten into trouble last night when we were beating into fifty-plus knots. That possibility makes me wonder how many sailors looked upon these rocks in their last few moments of consciousness and how many skeletal remains we are sailing over—metal, wood, and bone.

Ahead of us, Cape Horn rises almost sheer from the water in a thousand-foot-high cliff of loose scree and larger boulders. The cliff culminates in a series of vertical gray tubes resembling pipes on a gigantic organ. The rest of the island rolls down from this point to sea level, in some places gently and in some places steeply, creating the wedge shape we saw when we first glimpsed the island. We leave Cape Horn to port, speak the lighthouse, and head back to Caleta Martial, reaching the anchorage just before the wind roars out of the northwest at gale force.

Less than twenty-four hours later, we hand our lines to our friends Marlene and Reinhart, on the German boat *Adio*, tied up to the *Micalvi* in Puerto Williams. "Did you hear about the German sailboat?" they ask before we have even gotten our spring lines sorted. "It was lost with all hands two nights ago. All they recovered was the EPIRB."

Our 180-mile round-trip to Cape Horn and back took less than sixty hours. Long enough to reach a sailing milestone . . . or end a sailing dream.

54° 56′ S, 67° 37′ W

m/v *Micalvi*, Club de Yates
Puerto Williams, Chile

January 11, 2003

M OST of the time, I cannot believe we are actually going to do this. Even as I provision for a minimum of sixty days at sea and a maximum of ninety, even while I'm canning soups and stews in the pressure cooker to give us hearty meals, even while Evans hoists and checks all of our storm sails and sets up our drogues and parachute for easy deployment, my mind has managed to skirt around what it is we are about to do. But now, as I stare down at the pilot chart spread out in front of Evans on the navigation table, it all becomes real. We are about to embark on a 9,000-nautical-mile passage across the Southern Ocean.

I'm not even sure when we agreed to this voyage. But the decision to sail back south down the Chilean channels to the Beagle Channel and Cape Horn begged another question: Where to next?

We have worn out our welcome in Chile visa wise; but even if that weren't the case, we need a change of scenery. Having spent the last three summers in thermal underwear and the last two winters listening to rain, sleet, and snow drumming on the coach roof, we are eager to sail someplace where more than just our faces and hands will get tan. But where? Starting from the southern tip of South America, the options are limited. We are not ready to end our voyage, so returning up the Atlantic holds no appeal. That leaves the Southern Ocean.

The very words conjure up images from dozens of sailing books and Vendee Globe/Volvo videos. Giant Southern Ocean "graybeards" climbing higher and higher over the stern of the boat while a grim-faced helmsman grips the wheel. A tabular iceberg the size of an apartment block looming out of the fog while the captain desperately calls for a change of course. A wall of green water seething down the decks and sweeping the crew into the lifelines. I have cartwheeled with the Smeetons in *Tzu Hang* off Cape Horn and been dismasted between South Africa and Australia with Isabelle Autissier—in both cases not once but twice. We have talked to the crews of the eight cruising boats we know who have sailed these latitudes. One boat was rolled and dismasted. Two boats hit icebergs and almost lost their masts. Three boats were knocked down beyond the horizontal at least once. And just a month ago a cruising boat coming from Tahiti was lost 200 miles off Cape Horn. Yet we plan to leave the Beagle Channel and sail eastabout nonstop under South Africa to Fremantle, the port serving Perth, the capital city of western Australia.

The *Atlas of Pilot Charts* for the South Atlantic and the Indian Ocean makes frighteningly real what has until now been comfortingly abstract. Red lines lap upward from Cape Horn and wash over the southern tip of Africa. "This shows the percentage of significant wave heights over twelve feet," Evans says, tracing one of these lines. "From here, under South Africa, almost all the way to Australia we can expect to be in waves over twelve feet high from thirty to forty percent of the time." The dotted red line denoting the northernmost limit of drift ice loops up above 35° S north of the Falkland Islands and almost touches South Africa, on the other side of the Atlantic. The percentage of gales doubles between 40° and 50° S, and from 45° to 50° tends to be in the double digits. That translates to an average of one gale per week over the course of a two-month voyage.

Over the next hour, we sift our way through the complex information on the pilot charts, and our route takes shape. Our course will take us out the Beagle Channel and through the Straits of Le Maire, then we'll turn northeast to pass under the Falkland Islands in order to avoid the Falklands Current. We'll sail to between 40° and 42° S, then turn east, passing under Tristan de Cunha. If, after some 4,000 miles and our longest passage ever, all's well and we feel no need to stop in South Africa, we'll stay right around 40° S to pass under the Cape of Good Hope. This course splits the difference between the contrary Agulhas current and the easterly winds along the coast, and the northernmost limit of drift ice. Somewhere between 105° and 110° E, we'll turn north for Fremantle—far enough east to give us a reaching angle for the last 600 miles through the prevailing southeast winds. That's the theory.

But I understand all too well what the reality is likely to be on a two-month passage through the Roaring Forties.

So, why? Why are we doing this?

I have asked myself this question dozens of times even as I have been preparing for what I know will be the hardest passage we have ever made. The answers that come are totally unsatisfactory. But underlying these is a feeling that came over me watching a slide show by Brian Hancock, who sailed in several Whitbread races through these same waters. Image after image flashed on the screen, huge waves and flying spray and crews trying desperately to douse sails—all set to thundering music. The show captured the raw beauty, savage power, and awesome magnificence of the wild and lonely waters at the end of the Earth. It terrified me. But it has never let me go. I want to experience it. I want to see a giant wandering albatross, with its twelve-foot wingspan, swooping and soaring in our wake over those Southern Ocean graybeards.

If we'd never built a boat capable of such a passage, if we'd never found ourselves here, at the tail end of South America trying to decide where to go next, I never would have gotten past the dreaming stage. But we're here, with *Hawk*.

This isn't logic. These aren't reasons. But this feeling runs bone-deep, and that seems to be enough.

52° 48′ S, 57° 55′ W

Puerto Williams, Chile to Fremantle, Australia
3rd day of passage (about 50 miles southeast of the Falkland Islands)

January 19, 2003

1430. Long night and longer day—forereaching in 30–40 knots with gusts to 50. Big waves. Barometer at 966 millibars. At bottom now?

I sit at the navigation table, bracing myself against the rearing-up, plunging-down, slip-slidey motion. The pen jumps and skids across the page of the logbook, leaving barely legible words in its wake. My stomach heaves, and I close my eyes and drop my head down on top of the open log, swallowing convulsively. As soon as I can lift my head, I'm out of the seat and climbing the companionway steps. I stand under the hard dodger, sucking in the salty sea air in openmouthed gasps. I'm surrounded by seething pyramids of water scratching at the sky where the horizon should be.

The waves have grown into fierce white-capped gray walls since 0500, when I wrote in the log, *"Blowing hard but reasonably comfortable. Forereaching, heeled 20°, waves not too bad."* Hawk heels and accelerates as a gust catches her deeply reefed mainsail. She races recklessly up the next wave face, but just as she reaches the crest the wave breaks, checking her progress as it slams into her bow and sends a torrent of green water tumbling down her decks. Churning green and white fingers crawl up the glass on the hard dodger in front of me before rushing back to the side decks. The cold of the near freezing air and water starts me shivering, but I'm not ready to go back to the warmth of my bunk. I need to make sure *Hawk* is still handling things out here, that she doesn't need help from us.

We left the Beagle Channel three days ago. The Armada personnel at each of five different lighthouses asked us our destination and ETA (estimated time of arrival), and each paused for several seconds at my reply—"Australia, in about two months"—before wishing us excellent weather, safe sailing, good luck. A few hours later, we were racing through the Straits of Le Maire in pitch darkness chased by a 4-knot current and 30 knots of wind when the clouds ripped apart to reveal the bright eye of the moon. In its brilliant light, each jagged peak of the wild mountains of Tierra del Fuego stood silhouetted, swathed in silver snowfields. I said good-bye to Patagonia in that enchanted moment.

Now I'm saying hello to the Southern Ocean.

We left with a forecast for a gale in three days, the best we could hope for at these latitudes. The low-pressure system was supposed to remain moderate with a center pressure of 980 millibars, and was supposed to stay south of 55°, but the system took a hard left and went north of us while deepening

considerably. Instead of northwest winds up to thirty knots as forecast, we've had gale- to storm-force winds from straight up our course for the last eighteen hours.

From his bunk below me, Evans asks, "How're we doing?"

"Barometer's still dropping; wind's still on our nose, though it's down a bit. The waves still aren't breaking. *Hawk*'s getting up to three or four knots at times, but she seems happy enough fore-reaching."

Evans grunts, and I return to my bunk, cuddling into the three wool blankets and down sleeping bag, trying to stop the shivering, enduring—knowing that this storm, like all the others before it, must end sometime.

0300. After leveling off for two to three hours, barometer's dropping again!!! Now reads 959–NEVER seen it this low . . . Wind back to north quadrant. Yuck!

I can't see anything except for the occasional flash of white as a wave crest tumbles down a face with the wind shredding it to spume. Deprived of my sight, my other senses seem amplified, and I'm sure the wind is stronger, the waves more fierce, the motion worse.

Sick worry gnaws at my stomach. We know what happens when the barometer starts to rise from such a deep low. In these latitudes, the wind tends to be between ten and fifteen knots stronger on the rise than on the fall. We've seen stretches of fifty knots overnight. What will we get on the rise? Sixty knots? Seventy? What will the seas look like when these southwest-running monsters are crossed by hurricane-force southeast winds?

I want reassurance. I want options. I want information. But there's none of any of that to be had. There's only trust. In *Hawk*, in Evans, in myself. And in something else I don't dare to name.

Dawn light slowly leaches into the clearing sky. *Hawk's* decks and cockpit emerge in grainy black and white, the winches a blur against moving water, the mast and shrouds smears of gray brushing the lightening horizon. Color seeps slowly back, and with it come details of line and texture. And then I see a lone shape moving against the water. It swoops and turns, careens over a crest and disappears, soars up again and drifts down in front of a wave face. In the gathering light I see the splatter of white leaching onto its wings from its back and the thick yellow beak. My eyes tear as I recognize my first wandering albatross at play among Southern Ocean graybeards, its twelve-foot wingspan dwarfed by the waves.

"We never saw them when it got really bad," an experienced Southern Ocean sailor had told me. "Oh, they're quite happy in thirty knots and they don't mind forty, but they make themselves scarce if it's going to blow over fifty or so."

1000. Barometer bottomed out at 956!! at 0800. Wind shifted to E, then SE, now S. Barometer up to 963 millibars, wind moderating. Sailing again.

Puerto Williams, Chile to Fremantle, Australia
31st day of passage (about 400 miles south of
    South Africa)

February 16, 2003

I AM riding a horse through a wind-tossed cornfield on a hot summer night when the insistent chirp of my alarm reaches into my dream in the guise of a demented cricket. By the time my mind has recognized the alarm for what it is, the water rushing along the hull a few inches from my ear has replaced the rustling of the cornstalks, and the horse's cantering motion has merged with *Hawk*'s. But the heat remains, and it takes me a minute to place myself in the Southern Ocean, 400 miles south of South Africa and just past the halfway point to Fremantle, and to remember that when I got into my bunk we were running under the jib in gale-force winds.

I smile at that thought, because for the first time since leaving the Beagle Channel thirty-one days and 4,300 nautical miles ago, we are sailing fast downwind. Until now, we have experienced none of the screaming downwind conditions I expected to be the norm on this passage. One word describes our Southern Ocean experience so far: changeable. In our first ten days, we slammed into three easterly gales and were all but becalmed between them. The wind has been aft of the beam only a third of the time, and for most of that it has been light. We have rarely gone more than one watch without a major sail change except when forereaching in gales or totally becalmed. My shoulders and arms ache from manhandling all the sails three or four times a day on a pitching deck.

I expect Evans to grunt a good-night to me while he makes a beeline for his sea berth. We have become obsessive about our bunk time after being sleep-deprived for the last week. Three days of trying to keep the boat moving in less than seven knots of wind was followed by two days of close reaching in 25 knots with ten- to twelve-foot seas on the beam. In both cases, the waves made it close to impossible to move around the boat, to cook, or to sleep. So now, when Evans doesn't appear, I start to get worried. "Evans?" I call.

"Out here," he answers from the cockpit. "Come on up."

I clamber out of my bunk and automatically reach for my expedition-weight thermal underwear before the tropical quality of the air registers. In comparison to the near-freezing desert air of the Arctic that we've been breathing for the last month, this feels like steam in my lungs. Here we are, several hundred miles south of the northernmost limit of drift ice, in waters that until now have averaged temperatures in the mid- to high forties, and I feel as though I should be putting on shorts. I pull on splash pants and a waterproof jacket over my lightweight thermal underwear and climb up on deck.

Evans stands in the cockpit, one hand on the handgrip on the back of the hard dodger, his hair frosted white by the full moon. *Hawk* races along under the furled jib, weaving a broad silver-and-gold wake as she passes through the water. Her motion feels as tropical as the air, an exhilarating sashay as she surges forward on each wave without the sudden checks and wild gyrations I have come to associate with Southern Ocean swell. Despite the gale-force wind, the waves have moderated considerably since I went off watch. The scene feels surreal, as though we've been transported 20 degrees farther north for this one moonlit, balmy night. I understand why Evans has, for the first time on this passage, spent his entire watch on deck, and why he is reluctant to go to his bunk even now, when he is losing precious sleep time.

"So what is it with this weather?" I ask.

"Look at the instruments."

The true wind speed indicator flashes numbers between 35 and 45, and our speed through the water shows 8 to 10 knots. But the GPS readout of boat speed averages 12 to 14 knots, and the water temperature reads a steady 77 degrees. "Pretty weird," I say.

"We must be in a countercurrent to the Agulhas," Evans tells me. The mighty Agulhas current carries tropical water down South Africa's east coast and across the bottom of the continent before dissipating in the frigid waters of the Southern Ocean. Tonight a little meander seems to have made its way several hundred miles to reach us, bringing us a taste of tropical weather and a four-knot boost to our boat speed while flattening out the waves.

As with so many things on this passage, I never expected this little miracle of warm water in the cold Southern sea. As usual, I worried about all the wrong things before we left. Instead of obsessing about how we were going to handle heavy weather, I should have been worrying about how we were going to keep the boat moving in the inevitable patches of light air that follow the frontal passages. Neither of us anticipated how physically taxing we would find the constant sail handling. We both forgot that coastal sailing doesn't push the boat in the same way as passagemaking. Despite the hard miles in the Chilean channels, we had to deal with a number of small breakages in the first two weeks of this passage until *Hawk* was again in offshore trim. But we have so far managed to handle everything the Southern Ocean has thrown at us, and a few days ago we made the decision to continue on to Australia without a stop in South Africa.

Evans heads for the companionway. "I guess I'd better get some sleep." I step aside to let him pass. "By the way," he says, "don't bother watching out for icebergs tonight." He chuckles all the way to his berth.

40° 29' S, 95° 15' E

Puerto Williams, Chile to Fremantle, Australia
52nd day of passage (Southern Indian Ocean)

March 9, 2003

I AM so absolutely, totally, completely sick of this. Forty minutes ago I furled the jib and raised the staysail when the wind built to 30 knots. Now it's dropped to 20 knots, and the ten- to twelve-foot waves crashing into *Hawk* just forward of the beam have started checking her progress. She needs more sail. But I just did a sail change, and the wind *will* come back up, and I'm tired of it, sick of it, all of it.

After a week close reaching into 25 to 30 knots of wind, I am tired of moving around the decks like a crab with one hand on a grabrail every second. I'm sick of trying to cook while the boat corkscrews and falls out from under me. I've had it with snatching sleep between lurches and crashes, my back wedged against the bunk board, one knee drawn up into my chest and my muscles tensed to stabilize me against the 30-degree heel and the constant roll. I can't stand the sight of the pile of wet clothing sitting on my desk waiting for a dry, downwind day that just never seems to come. We haven't seen the sun in ten days, haven't sailed downwind in moderate breezes in two weeks. Worst of all, after fifty-two days at sea—twenty-three days longer than our longest passage before this—we still have more than a thousand miles of Southern Ocean ahead of us.

Another violent lurch, then a voice from down below: "She feels like she needs more sail."

Yeah, right. What does he know? *He's* been sleeping, *I'm* the one who's on watch. "She's fine. The wind's just up and down a little. Go back to sleep."

But the wind's staying around twenty knots. I'll give it five more minutes, then maybe I'll switch to the jib. And what do you want to bet that I'll be changing back again in an hour if I do that?

Darn. Ten minutes and the wind's steady at 20 knots. I really will have to add some sail. And, of course, here comes that voice again: "She really feels as if she wants more sail."

"All right, all right. I'll drop the staysail and put up the jib. But don't blame me if we have to furl the jib back up in an hour."

"Do you want any help?"

What am I supposed to say?

"No. I'll take care of it." Now why couldn't he have just come up here? But no, he has to ask, and I can't tell him he has to get out of that nice, warm, comfortable bunk, get all kitted up into foul-weather gear, come out on deck and get soaking wet, then go back below and try to get to sleep again. How exasperating. I wouldn't behave that way. Well . . . okay, I have been behaving *exactly* that way when I'm off watch. But from now on I'll be right out of that bunk when he needs me. . . . Yeah, right.

Let's see if we can do this without getting wet. Clip my tether to the jackline. Grab three sail ties, scuttle forward. . . . Oops, here comes a big wave. Hold on, duck. . . . Missed me. Here we are. Uncoil the line, release the halyard. Pull down the sail. Attach the lanyard to the headboard. Back to the mast . . . oh, grab that handrail! That was a nice little jolt, *Hawk*. Thanks a lot.

Cleat off the halyard. Sit down on the side deck, wedge my feet against the toe rail and grab the sail. . . . If I can reach just a bit farther . . .

OH! Oh is that cold! Half the ocean just went right down my neck. Everything I'm wearing is soaked—again. Great, just great. Why am I up here doing this? Evans didn't have to do a single sail change on his last watch, and look at me. I do *all* the sail changes. And he's getting a lot more sleep than I am. Why he's been down there for two full hours. I haven't slept two hours straight in at least three days. Well, maybe I did get almost three hours on my last off watch, and I do remember Evans making several sail changes during his watch yesterday. But he does a lot less than I do. I do the sail handling and the cooking and the cleaning up and . . .

There. Last sail tie on. Let's see if I can get out of here without getting soaked again. Okay, unfurl the jib. Boat speed's back up. Seven knots, seven and a half. Spray flying everywhere again, but at least she's not wallowing.

The voice again: "She feels better. Everything all right?"

"Fine, just fine. I got soaking wet when an entire wave jumped down the collar of my foul-weather jacket, but other than that everything's just great."

"You sound cranky. I think you need some sleep."

"Cranky? Me, cranky? What do you mean? I'm just fine. You're the one who won't let me handle my own watch."

"You need some sleep." His voice has taken on a tone I know very well, one that means we're going to have a nice little fight in about two minutes.

Fine by me. "What are we doing out here anyway? Whose idea was this? Not mine, I can tell you that."

"As I recall, I suggested heading across the Pacific last year. Remember? Trade winds, warm water, no clothes?"

And I do remember. This was my choice. But after fifty-two days I've had it. I am so sick of gray. Gray sky, gray sea, gray boat, gray thoughts. And I remember Evans asking a Whitbread veteran about what a Southern Ocean passage was like. "It's all shades of gray," he had answered cryptically. Now I understand.

Which doesn't help in the slightest.

Puerto Williams, Chile to Fremantle, Australia
59th day of passage (12 miles southwest
of entrance to Fremantle Harbour)

March 16, 2003

We are half a world from where we started.

After fifty-nine days at sea, the southwest coast of Australia lies off to starboard, a blurred strand of yellow and orange lights strung across the eastern horizon. Since we last saw land, we have sailed almost 9,000 nautical miles, made close to three hundred sail changes, and crossed eleven time zones. I cannot take it in. Not the sudden explosion of man-made light into our tiny world, nor the idea that we have made landfall. This voyage is about to come to an end. But like Australia itself, that thought is too big to grasp. I cannot get hold of it.

What am I feeling? Not the normal jubilation I have come to associate with landfall, that adrenaline-fueled surge of excitement and anticipation. Nor do I feel the strange ambivalence that often accompanies the end of a passage, the tug-of-war between wanting to arrive and wanting to continue—of not wanting to break the rhythm of passagemaking and give up the elegant simplicity and vivid immediacy of life at sea. After two months offshore, there is no question that I am ready for this passage to end. Over the last ten days, Evans and I have been rubbing up against each other in ways that irritate and annoy. I cannot wait to step off the boat and have some space, both mental and physical. I cannot wait to feel my leg muscles stretch and grow sore on a long walk ashore. I cannot wait to get more than three or four hours of sleep at a time. I cannot wait for my world to be quiet and still.

I want this passage to be over, but now that it's ending I am empty of emotion, out of words.

I came on watch an hour ago to find the lights of Fremantle on the horizon and Evans preoccupied. Before he went below to get some sleep, we took down the spinnaker pole. We moved with the ease of familiarity, not a word spoken between us. Our bodies swayed to the roll of the boat, our hands flitted without thought from pole to handgrip and back, the dance of our motions choreographed by the rhythm of the sea. Sometime in the last two months, we have become part of *Hawk*, our movements—like hers—an extension of the sea's motion. And somewhere along the way, emotion seems to have seeped away and been replaced by *Hawk*'s calm acceptance and the stoicism of the sea.

> *Sometime in the last two months, we have become part of* Hawk, *our movements—like hers—an extension of the sea's motion. And somewhere along the way, emotion seems to have seeped away and been replaced by* Hawk's *calm acceptance and the stoicism of the sea.*

Earlier today Evans took a blue marker and traced the line of our passage on the map of the world mounted on *Hawk*'s cabin bulkhead. Looking at that thin blue line brought back all of the fears and misgivings I had at the beginning of this voyage. But we were incredibly fortunate. Ellen MacArthur's catamaran, *Kingfisher*, got towed through these waters and into the port ahead of us just a few days ago. Her run at the Jules Verne trophy ended when the cat was dismasted near the Kergulen Islands in the Southern Ocean. Friends who left the Beagle Channel ten days ahead of us just sent us an e-mail saying they'd been rolled 30 degrees past the horizontal, taken on a great deal of water, and come close to sinking the boat. But our passage has, all in all, been uneventful.

I don't feel proud of that. The sea was kind; it could just as easily have been otherwise. I miss the albatross. They grew scarce as we turned north and left the Roaring Forties behind, disappearing altogether once we passed 35° S. My last visitor stayed for several hours, a spectacular, almost totally white wandering albatross that may well have been older than I. He moved with majesty, not flicking so much as a feather as he wove back and forth in our wake, then soared off over our bow to return five minutes later to our stern. Huge black clouds hung in the sky behind him, but the sun shone off to port, causing the turning waves to flash with the cerulean blue of glaciers under their lace of white spume. And in front of the waves, my old warrior friend looped and glided, almost touching a foaming crest with a wing tip before tucking up and over and into the trough beyond. When he soared away, he left us alone on an achingly empty ocean.

A light flashes from the darkness dead over *Hawk*'s bow—Rottnest Island, just north of the channel we will take through the reefs and islands paralleling the coast to reach the harbor at Fremantle. I drop down the companionway and wake Evans. A few minutes later he comes up on deck, and together we watch the light grow closer, the end of the passage draw nearer. Neither of us speaks, but with Evans's presence come the first curling tendrils of emotion.

I feel . . . privileged. Relieved. Humbled. Awed. I feel grateful to be here, with *Hawk* still in fine shape and Evans and I still friends and partners in the adventure that is our lives. And . . . I feel bemused. I still cannot believe we chose to do this passage, even less that we have actually done it.

I have been polished to granite by the constant wash of the sea, worn away to my essence, transported to a place beyond emotion and thought. What will it take to return to shore life, to let go of the sea now pulsing in my veins, to put this passage behind me?

Will I begin to feel again in a few hours, when we tie up to the customs dock? Maybe it will happen when I am surrounded by Australian accents, or see traffic on the "wrong" side of the street, or sip a Foster's lager, or see a kangaroo. Or maybe I'll never return to shore in the same way I have before.

41° 01' N, 73° 34' W

s/v *Ginny* near Rowayton, Connecticut
Long Island Sound, USA

July 25, 2003

FOR the last week I have been seeing ghosts. Or, to be accurate, a ghost. Out of the corner of my eye, I think I see Walker's small, neat hands on the wheel below his tanned, boyish face as he watches his wife, Ginny, and I flake the mainsail. But when I turn and look directly at the stern, there's no one there.

Ever since I arrived in Southport, Connecticut, and spotted the Cal 39 *Ginny* in her berth at the yacht club a week ago, I have been seeing Walker. I saw him waving to me from *Ginny*'s cockpit as I walked across the close-cropped lawn of the club, past the stately colonial brick building where he and I spent many hours talking about *Hawk* and about *Ginny*, then only boats-to-be. When I stepped on board, he stood by the traveler coiling the mainsheet and telling me how much better it was now that he had added a 16:1 tackle for fine-tuning. When I started below to stow my duffel bag, he looked up from the stripped interior and smiled, pausing before fitting the next pine batten into the new ceiling he was installing. When I dropped my duffel, disoriented, and sat down at the nav table, I felt Walker's shoulder against mine while he flashed digital images on his computer screen of the season that he and Ginny had spent cruising the Caribbean aboard this boat.

But I actually sat with Walker at *Ginny*'s nav station a year ago. And Walker Vought died less than a month after that, on September 9, 2002. The fast-growing and virulent cancer invading his brain even then, when we were looking at pictures of Guadeloupe and the Virgins, gave him no time to fight. And it left his wife and lover, Ginny, adrift without a partner and, to a certain extent, without a life. A year before, they had cut their ties to shore and gone cruising, leaving everything open-ended. "We'll do the Caribbean for a year and see how we like it. Then we'll decide what comes next." Neither of them could possibly have foreseen what did come next.

In the ten months following Walker's death, I have spoken to Ginny as often as time zones and phone access have allowed. She has been slowly redefining her life, trying to fill the gaping hole that once could barely contain Walker, with all his boundless energy and contagious enthusiasm for sailing, for people, for life. Sometime last November she told me she had decided to go cruising again, to try it for a year, and we fantasized about sailing together when I was next in the country. I flew back to the States from Fremantle, Australia, at the end of June to spend six weeks visiting family and friends. Now, here I am—aboard the boat that Walker so lovingly refit—at the end of Ginny's first week as skipper.

Ginny has spent most of her time aboard this boat since just after the funeral when she and her daughters scattered Walker's ashes on Long Island Sound. Over the winter, in addition to resolving the myriad details always left dangling by a sudden death, she had a new engine installed, learned coastal navigation, painted the bottom—trying to bridge the huge gap between being half of a cruising partnership and managing a boat single-handed. Ginny has all the skills she needs to make the transition. She began sailing before she knew how to walk, and she is one of the few women I know who has sailed single-handed on occasion. But she lacks confidence in her mechanical skills and navigational skills, and, most of all, she lacks the confidence necessary to make a decision when it might put lives at risk.

When I arrived a week ago, she looked smaller and frailer than I remembered. Always petite, with platinum blond hair and fair skin, she seemed to have lost the inner dynamism that invested her small frame with a glowing vitality. The skin was drawn tightly across her cheekbones, and when I folded her into my arms I felt as though I was an oversized coat into which she might disappear.

The week we have spent together has been a whirlwind. We have been up and sailing just after dawn most mornings, sailed through the early afternoon, then worked on the boat before collapsing into bed around eleven at night. We have replaced corroded connections on electrical equipment, fixed latches and hatches, discussed sail combinations for various wind speeds and conditions, practiced anchoring techniques, tried out storm sails. One thing always led to another, until we found ourselves with four projects going on at once and the boat torn up from one end to the other. Through it all we talked a lot, laughed a lot, and cried a little.

All week Walker has been here with us. I keep catching sight of him just as he disappears up the companionway or slips into the forepeak. Ginny sometimes pauses in the middle of a thought as if listening to a voice I cannot hear, or tears come to her eyes when she picks up something small and seemingly insignificant, such as a half-finished bottle of shampoo. We talk about him because we want to, need to, because it brings him even closer. Ginny told me how grateful she was that she and Walker had their Caribbean interlude; that he got to fulfill his dream.

And I watched her steadily increasing confidence as she reefed the main in 25 knots with spray scudding over the decks; threaded the boat through the twists and turns of narrow Mattituck Inlet, on Long Island; and felt her way into the Coast Guard station at Eatons Neck. She became comfortable telling me what we were going to do, then giving me orders as we did it. Now as we flake the sail for the last time before heading back to her mooring on the river at Rowayton—and what will be a difficult farewell—I notice the red flush in her cheeks over the bronzed skin, feel the strength of her as she levers the sail tie against the boom, and know she is going to be all right.

We finish flaking the sail in Bristol fashion. "Walker approves," we say together, then look at each other and laugh. Back at the helm, I catch the flash of a smile, though perhaps it is just the sun skipping over a wave.

Bunbury to Albany, Western Australia

October 1, 2003

I HUDDLE under the hard dodger in the darkness, shivering with cold, my stomach roiling. Neither the three layers of thermal underwear nor the seasickness medications I took seem to be making the slightest bit of difference. For the thousandth time that night, I feel *Hawk* rear up, then crash down, and hear the waterfall rush of the sea as it races by me along the side deck before cascading off the stern. I tell myself I have to get up and check our position, but I know that only if I stay absolutely still will I keep from being sick. I have to fight my way past my body's protective instincts and through the overwhelming apathy that engulfs me just to engage my muscles.

When I manage it, I swing my legs off the cockpit seat and stand, swallowing repeatedly to control the nausea. The instruments over the companionway tell me we still have five miles to go to the waypoint, and the wind remains dead up our course at 18 to 22 knots true. I haul myself back onto the cockpit seat and scan the horizon in all directions. I see only the heaving dark masses of water against the darker sky, and the flashes of white from the turning crests. I think I just might make it back to my seat under the dodger without getting sick, but I am wrong.

Twelve hours earlier, we left Cape Leeuwin to port. Named for the Dutch ship that discovered it, Leeuwin means "lioness" and is one of the sailors' three "Great Capes." Despite its name, Leeuwin lacks the fearsome reputation of Cape Horn or the Cape of Good Hope, yet it lies almost a degree south of Hope.

And, like Hope, it is located not at the southernmost extent of the continent but at its most southwestern point, the place where square-rigged sailing vessels fighting the westerly winds could finally ease sheets and turn northward.

We were coming in the opposite direction to those sailing ships of yore and would have been glad to have some of those westerly winds. A little over a week before, we had left our winter berth in Fremantle and headed south. We reached Bunbury, a small port town halfway between Perth and Cape Leeuwin, and waited there for five days hoping for a favorable forecast. But once the summer high-pressure systems become established in the Australian bight, the prevailing winds along the southern coast of Australia switch from westerly to easterly. Local sailors and the pilot charts agreed we could round Leeuwin and cross the bight on westerly winds when the last of the winter fronts passed through in October or November, but by December the window would slam shut and we could expect almost nonstop easterlies.

We arrived in Bunbury in late September prepared to wait. But this is the first time we've ever left somewhere with a mobile phone aboard, allowing us to remain in close contact with the friends we left behind. When the first caller expressed surprise that we were still in Bunbury, I told her we might be there for several weeks and said, "It is a Great Cape after all." But after having the same conversation half a dozen times, we began to feel pressured. The breaking point came when we got a forecast for four days of southeast winds of eight to twelve knots and our friends Bob and Jacquie called. New cruisers who had left Fremantle aboard their 39-foot sloop, *Isalei-Rua*, the same time as we did, they were waiting at an anchorage farther south. "What do you think?" Bob asked.

"It's as good a forecast as you can expect without it being westerly." I knew that if it was westerly it would likely be blowing a gale, and I understood their reluctance to deal with heavy weather around Leeuwin on their first real passage.

"We're leaving," Bob said.

We preferred riding a downwind gale around Leeuwin, but we let the social pressure get to us. Twelve hours later we rounded our third Great Cape aboard *Hawk*. But instead of the light easterly winds we'd been enjoying along the last bit of the west coast, we came around the corner to find 20- to 25-knot southeast winds. Eight-foot swells rolling in from the Southern Ocean in addition to the six- to eight-foot-high wind-driven waves made these headwinds more than uncomfortable.

The next available shelter for *Hawk* lay at Albany, 175 miles to the southeast. If we'd been aboard *Silk*, the 37-foot ketch we circumnavigated in, we wouldn't even have tried to continue. We would have run back around Leeuwin to a safe anchorage. But it's *Hawk's* blessing and her curse that she sails upwind far better than we do. Now that we had Leeuwin to port, the pressure we'd been feeling for almost a week made the decision for us. Besides, we reasoned, the forecast couldn't be completely wrong. The wind would drop—probably in an hour or so.

Twelve hours later, as *Hawk* slams down with a force that shakes her rigging, I can't believe we've been so stupid.

It takes us another twenty-four miserable, seasick hours to reach Albany. The wind never eases, and with every small course change it shifts just enough to remain dead on the nose. We are feeling battered and bruised when we finally drop the anchor under the sand dunes at Princess Royal Harbour.

We don't even try to explain when friends from Fremantle express surprise that we found 20 to 25 knots of wind so unpleasant. But when Jacquie calls almost in tears from the tiny anchorage where they managed to take shelter after making good only 65 miles in 36 hours, I say, "Don't think this is cruising. This is misery."

Two days later we wake to westerly winds.

Albany, Western Australia to Port Davey, Tasmania
5th day of passage

October 18, 2003

W E'RE waiting.

Five days out to sea and more than 850 nautical miles south-east of Albany, on the south coast of Australia, we're well into the Roaring Forties in early spring. The sky has taken on the texture of a fisherman's sweater, winnowed rows of coarse slate-colored wool unraveling into wispy tendrils that brush the surface of the pewter sea. The barometer has been dropping sharply for the last four hours after dropping slowly for twelve. A long swell out of the southwest some ten to twelve feet high clashes with the waves kicked up by the gale-force northeast wind we had overnight. Here wave and swell combine into a lopsided pyramid towering over *Hawk*'s stern; there they crash into one another and collapse into a welter of white on the sea's surface. Sea and sky tell us that soon—ten minutes? an hour? two hours?—the front will be upon us. But this morning's forecast told us much more: we're at the start of three days of worsening weather culminating in twelve to twenty-four hours of forty-plus-knot westerly winds with gusts up to sixty knots and average wave heights of twenty feet.

For now, though, we're waiting.

We've done everything we can to prepare. We already have a dozen sail ties on the main; the boom is secured and the checkstays are up; everything below has been stowed and all the lockers locked; the warps for the drogue are ready to run and the drogue is accessible. Evans is trying to get some sleep.

There's nothing else to do now but wait.

I feel the coming weather in the pressure in my ears and the dull ache at the back of my head, in the hollow sensation where my stomach should be and the bunched muscles in my shoulders and neck. I'm not afraid, not exactly. I know the three of us can handle what has been forecast; we've handled that and more. But anytime the seas get up to that windblown spume, streaky white state, forecasts tell you only so much, and preparation and experience go only so far. At the extreme, we're one wave, one mistake away from crossing the fine line between okay and not, between upright and over, between whole and injured.

I'm not afraid, not exactly. I know the three of us can handle what has been forecast; we've handled that and more. But anytime the seas get up to that windblown spume, streaky white state, forecasts tell you only so much, and preparation and experience go only so far. At the extreme, we're one wave, one mistake away from crossing the fine line between okay and not, between upright and over, between whole and injured.

From the vantage point of a small boat at sea, I've come to understand why Admiral Beaufort and generations of sailing ship captains considered that gale-force winds begin somewhere over 30-ish knots. A 20-knot, 25-knot, or even 30-knot sea is a series of individual waves, many with whitecaps, each easily surmountable on any point of sail by any well-found vessel. But between 30 and 40 knots, the sea starts to change. The forces between individual waves begin to interact, and the added dynamic of swell or current creates dangerous cross seas or sudden, unpredictable eruptions of water. The waves themselves become interlinked, the largest often coming in groups of two or three. When average wave heights reach 15 to 20 feet, we will see some 40-foot waves, large enough to be a danger to the boat if caught on the beam. At the same time, the force on the sails goes

from pressed to loaded. Everything on board is bar tight and humming, and if gear fails—a sheet snaps or a block breaks—control can turn to chaos in less time than it takes to blink.

Standing in the companionway watching the heaving silver and gray fabric of the sea, I feel vulnerable. Once the wind has blown at gale force for several hours, luck will begin to play a larger role in our continued well-being than it normally does on the boat. Ashore, bad luck often blindsides us and good luck frequently goes unnoticed; we rarely wake up Monday morning without an accurate picture in our heads of how the week will end. But I am fully aware that I have no way of knowing what will happen in the next few days. Having handled heavy weather before, I can picture putting out a drogue or hand steering during big waves or trying to sleep in my bunk. But almost everything we do in the next day—or two, or even three—will be reactive, and the amount within our control will decrease by a tiny fraction with each hour of gale-force winds. One rogue wave or one broken piece of gear could turn a few minutes out of these coming days into a watershed in our lives.

The odds are, though, that nothing untoward will happen. The forecast conditions are not that extreme; we are experienced; *Hawk* is strong and seaworthy. But from now until the seas subside, Evans and I will exist in a state of heightened awareness, a sort of alert anxiety. When we first started sailing, I thought I would get over this feeling with enough heavy-weather experience. Now I know that this feeling is part of why we sail and one of the reasons we continue to sail safely.

The sky behind us has turned black and bruised; the unraveling clouds now meet the sea in a curtain of rain. The first few drops splatter on the deck. A wall of wind races toward us, pushing up furrows of white-capped wavelets on the surface of the waves. When it reaches us, *Hawk* surges forward as if she's been lashed, leaving a swirl of whitewater in her wake.

The waiting is at an end.

43° 20' S, 146° 06' E

Horseshoe Inlet, Bathurst Harbour
Port Davey, Tasmania

October 29, 2003

I STAND in an undulating springtime landscape of skeletal gray and dusky green under the upthrust heads of rocky peaks. Beneath me, a broad ribbon of blue cleaves the land, widening and narrowing as it meanders across my field of vision. Several hundred feet above me, the bright yellow of Evans's rain jacket dips and weaves across a rock outcropping, a vivid contrast to the muted high-latitude colors. A patch of blue sky appears overhead, but heavy clouds are again rolling in from the west trailing long gray wisps of rain. My eyes seek out the slender column of *Hawk*'s mast poking up from behind the only coppice of tall trees in view, looking small and fragile in this outsize landscape.

When seen on a map of Tasmania, the fjord-like complex of harbors, bays, and channels that make up Port Davey and Bathurst Harbour appears as clenched jaws under a hooked nose at the southwest corner of the island. Covering some 250 square miles, the entire area lies within the Southwest National Park, one of three interlinked parks that make up close to 20 percent of Tasmania's landmass. The whole has been designated a UNESCO World Heritage site to protect some of the last temperate rain forests left in the world. During the summer, tourists arrive aboard planes to explore the fjord in tour boats. But in early spring, Port Davey can be accessed only by several days of rugged overland hiking or by boat from the Southern Ocean.

Five days ago, after running with a drogue for twenty-four hours before gale- to storm-force winds, we surfed into Port Davey in twenty-foot seas and ducked into the lee of the aptly named Breaksea Island. We found ourselves in flat-calm water covered with white spume from the breakers dashing themselves to spindrift in hundred-foot plumes against the island's windward side. Since then, gale-force winds and heavy rains have kept us virtually boatbound. When the weather eased off this morning, we were eager to stretch our legs and do some exploring. Two hours of arduous walking up the steep hills warmed me while causing muscles made stiff and slow by a couple of weeks' close confinement to stretch and burn.

Now I stand gazing out over the landscape, using the scenery as an excuse to rest my legs and catch my breath. Evans works his way back down the steep slope to me and points to the curtain of gray descending over the hills across the channel from us. "If we head down now, we can get back to the boat without getting wet."

It is impossible to move fast, especially downhill. Dense bushes with spiky knee-high branches rise out of spongy, ankle-deep moss, and with each step I have to feel my way down to something solid, careful not to end up with my weight on my ankle instead of the bottom of my foot. Where the soil has been eroded away, coarse, slippery grass threatens to send me sliding down the slope. In the flat areas between the ridges, where the almost-continuous rains have pooled into soupy bogs, oozy black mud threatens to pull a boot right off. Wherever possible, we follow the bare rock along the ridgelines and avoid the low land between, but at times the only way across is to slog right through. Before we are halfway down, my boots are waterlogged and I have gone from sweating to shivering.

By the time we reach the level ground half a mile or so from the channel, the sky has darkened, the temperature has dropped ten degrees, and the building wind has whipped long blue-black shadows into the surface of the water. The first fat drops of rain splatter onto the rocks as we climb into the dinghy. In *Hawk*'s cockpit, we step out of our hiking boots and sling our rain jackets on the winches under the hard dodger. Just as I slide open the companionway, the wind rattles the halyards at the top of the mast, and sheets of rain cascade over the dodger windows.

Evans and I drop down the companionway steps into the warmth from the diesel heater. The aroma of fresh-baked bread fills the boat; on the counter sit the golden loaves I pulled from the oven just before our walk. I close the companionway, and the pounding rain becomes a muffled drumming while the howling wind turns into a low keening note in the rigging. The serene coziness of the cabin envelops us, made all the more secure and comfortable by the distant clamor from the tempest raging outside.

When the time comes and we have to give up this cruising life, this is what I will miss the most. I will miss the sun-dappled, aquamarine moments spent anchored near reefs; the driving-downwind days, making miles on passage; the fun-filled hours exploring a small village ashore; the energizing interactions with local people the world over; the magical meetings with sailing friends in distant anchorages; and the awesome experience of sailing in front of a glacier face. But what I will miss the most is both simpler and more complex than any of these. It is the time spent in a remote place, made possible by voyaging in a small boat, the self-sufficiency we enjoy in that place, and the cozy contentment to be found in *Hawk*'s cabin on a cold, wet, windy day.

43° 11′ S, 147° 17′ E

D'Entrecasteaux Channel, Tasmania
About 20 miles south of Hobart

February 24, 2004

THE water whispers softly as *Hawk*'s bow parts it, the tiny ripples spreading outward in a V over the black-mirrored surface behind us. I just barely feel the warm breath of the zephyr on my cheek as I stand on the coaming looking for any stirring of the flat calm in the channel ahead of us. A hundred yards to windward, a racy 35-foot sloop tacks in slow motion, heading toward the ruffled water along the western shore. The little blue catboat with its varnished wooden mast will cross us in another fifteen minutes; the two gray heads of her crew are just visible above her gunwales. "They're gaining on us," Evans says.

Yesterday we left Hobart and enjoyed a fast downwind sail in a strong northeast breeze fifteen miles south to the D'Entre-casteaux Channel, which lies between the Tasmanian mainland and 30-mile-long Bruny Island. Located on the southeast corner of Tasmania, the D'Entrecasteaux and its interlinked rivers, channels, and harbors make up the largest, most accessible, and most sheltered of the island's various cruising grounds. Along its banks, dozens of anchorages and a half dozen small towns nestle into low, rolling hills covered in eucalypt forests, all backed by the higher mountains of the Tasman interior. Cruising anywhere in this compact area, we are never more than an hour away from a good anchorage or a long daysail away from the "big smoke" of the capital city, Hobart.

Two hours ago, Evans raised the mainsail, then sheeted in the boom as I raised the anchor, and *Hawk* glided silently across Barnes Bay, the sheltered inner harbor at the northern end of Bruny Island. We tacked our way out of the harbor into 6 knots of true wind enjoying all the small noises that *Hawk* makes under way—sounds usually lost to the engine's clatter or the whining wind and whooshing seas. The water chuckled along her sides; the sail material rustled softly as it tacked through the rigging; the sheet creaked as the sail filled on the new tack. When I sheeted in the sail, the winch's rattle sounded shatteringly loud in the hushed silence. The sun grew pleasantly warm on my bare arms, a sensual summer feeling barely remembered after three years of thermal underwear sailing.

As we came into the D'Entrecasteaux, the wind bent by 90 degrees and dropped to a scant 4 knots. We found ourselves in company with two other boats tacking south into the zephyr's soft breath, toward a dogleg in the channel some five miles away. Seeing their crews working as hard as we were to keep their boats moving well, Evans chuckled. "Definition of a sailboat race: two boats with sails up within sight of each other."

So far, we haven't disgraced ourselves. In the last twenty minutes, the wind has dropped still further, and the instruments are showing only 1 or 2 knots of apparent wind. *Hawk* is making 3 to 4 knots over the bottom sailing at 28 degrees to the apparent wind, and we have held our own against the sloop. The catboat now has the advantage, sailing higher and faster than we are.

"Ease the outhaul," Evans says from the helm. "That's good. Almost two knots of boat speed. But we're still not pointing high enough."

He drops down onto the coaming where he can see the telltales on the jib. He brings *Hawk* up gently—3 degrees, 5 degrees, 8 degrees—until the wind instruments say we are sailing within less than ten degrees of the apparent wind. The telltales start to flutter and he falls off a tiny bit. I ease the mainsheet until the luff of the mainsail shudders, then I sheet it in ever so slightly. It's a lesson we learned before but have forgotten in too many miles with an excess of wind. In these conditions, we have to sail the boat like a dinghy, ignoring the instruments completely, feeling the wind, watching the sails, coaxing the last small bit of forward motion out of the boat. Sailing, just sailing.

Tasmania does not have any glaciers. Its mountains are less than half the height of the Andes. It hasn't got the castles of Scotland, the pubs of Ireland, or the raw volcanic power of Iceland. But it does offer the kind of cruising to be found in only a dozen or so places around the globe, places such as Penobscot Bay in Maine, Notre Dame Bay in Newfoundland, the Inner Hebrides in Scotland, and Bay of Islands in New Zealand. After three years of demanding offshore passages and stressful high-latitude coastal cruising, Evans, *Hawk*, and I were ready for a real summer and some real sailing. Not trying to get anywhere in particular, not worrying about seasons and weather windows, not always having to move the boat efficiently under sail or power—just being here, now, in the bright sunshine under *Hawk*'s white wings.

The catboat crosses just behind our stern, and we all lean back and relax, pretending we aren't trying to get every hundredth of a knot out of our boats. "Good'ay!" "How ya' goin'?" We have almost reached the headland at the dogleg when a broad, dark shadow races across the water toward us. I am at the mast before it hits, easing the halyard to tuck in a reef. *Hawk* drops her shoulder and charges, and Evans laughs as I pull in the reefing lines. By the time I'm finished, we've rounded the point and our two companions have disappeared, scattered by the wind.

No worries, mate. We're in Tassie, land of Oz, down under down under. And we're just cruisin'.

Hobart, Tasmania to Bay of Islands, New Zealand
8th day of passage

March 19, 2004

STARS upon stars upon stars. Above me, below me, all around me. Bold stars spin outward in knotted spirals from the Milky Way; a faint mist of stars lies suspended in the gossamer webs of the Magellanic clouds; twinkling stars sparkle across the black-mirrored surface of the sea. As my eyes slowly adjust to the darkness, more and yet more stars appear until they fill every space I'd thought empty, some hard as diamonds and cold as ice, others as indistinct as the blur of snowflakes in a blizzard. *Hawk* soars across the middle of a star-filled sphere, and only an occasional spark of brilliant phosphorescence among the stars' myriad reflections reveals the surface of the water beneath us, as black and opaque as the infinity of space.

I have never seen the ocean so calm. This can't possibly be the tempestuous Tasman Sea.

We left Tasmania a week ago bound for Opua, on the North Island of New Zealand. We were not looking forward to this passage, for everyone we know who has sailed high latitudes regards the Tasman as one of the roughest, stormiest, most fickle stretches of water in the world. Weather systems whirl in from three directions to collide in the sea between Australia and New Zealand. Southern Ocean storms sweep across the Roaring Forties; the remnants of tropical cyclones swoop down out of the Coral Sea; and low-pressure bombs develop off the southeast coast of Australia before rocketing eastward toward New Zealand.

It was one of the latter that hit friends aboard a Waterline 48 a month ago in these waters. The evening weatherfax had shown a weak low-pressure system with an associated front and had forecast a 30-knot shift to the southwest. *Red*, a well-built, solid, 48-foot steel cutter, was making good progress under a double-reefed main and staysail into 25 knots of northeast wind, with our friend Peter Cook on watch and her owner, Kevin Hansen, sound asleep below. Peter has half a dozen Sydney-to-Hobart races to his credit and is no stranger to big winds. He heard a sound like jet engines and saw what looked like a wall of smoke approaching from behind.

He just managed to disengage the autopilot and take the helm before the boat was hit by wind the likes of which he'd never experienced before. It took him and Kevin close to two hours to douse the sails and run off under bare poles trailing warps. At that point, they were composed enough to get out a video recorder. We saw the videotape the night before we left Hobart. After panning to the wind instruments to show them recording more than seventy knots apparent, the camera switched to Kevin, his face grim as he worked the helm. His economical movements looked comical in comparison with the fast-forward speed of the white-whipped waves behind him, rearing up, tilting sideways, collapsing, or exploding into bursts of spindrift and spume. The instruments recorded a peak gust of 86 knots apparent; for about four hours the true winds were in excess of seventy knots.

Although their experience was extreme, few people we know who have crossed the Tasman have managed it without some kind of drama. But in the last week, strong high-pressure systems in the Australian bight and over New Zealand have freeze-framed the weather and left us in a massive meteorological hole. We've had winds over ten knots only once, for about six hours. The wind has stayed well forward of the beam, so for most of the passage we have been able to make progress under our working sails, ghosting along at three to four knots in about the same amount of true wind across increasingly flat water. A few hours ago, our wind instruments read 0.0 knots for perhaps the first time ever at sea, and we decided to motor. Now I have come on watch to a sea as calm as any I have ever seen and to a sky given unbelievable depth and texture by layer upon layer of stars.

The Milky Way has always looked like a whitish mist to me, but tonight I see individual stars and nebulae and galaxies, their outlines smeared by unimaginable distances. These combine to make up the scales of a sinuous snake, twisting and twirling across the arc of the sky to enmesh the Southern Cross in its coils. The blizzard of stars in the Milky Way appears a million times more distant than the two brightest stars in the Cross, both vivid blue. I am rendered insignificant by the limitless reaches of space and the vast expanses of time that light has crossed to be imprinted on my retina. The star-filled sphere through which *Hawk* flies has no edge and no end that I am capable of comprehending.

This sky is no planetarium projection, and I am not at its center. It pulls me out of myself and forces me to glimpse, for the briefest of moments, what a pale, faded, limited imitation of reality I take as truth. The very act of comparison brings me back into myself, and my vision narrows to a pinprick. I'm left with nothing more than a distant echo of a transcendent reality that I struggle to put into words.

I feel as I did when we crossed our outbound track and finished our circumnavigation aboard *Silk*. After sailing each day for more than two years toward the setting sun we knew—not just intellectually but in the fiber of our beings—that the world *was* round when we ghosted under the headlands of English Harbour, in Antigua, and ended up back where we had started.

Hobart, Tasmania to Bay of Islands, New Zealand
Landfall on 9th day of passage

March 21, 2004

Come on, Beth. Wake up. I need your help."
I groan and roll over. I become aware of *Hawk*'s easy motion and remember we are on passage, closing with Cape Reinga, on the northern end of New Zealand's North Island, nine days after leaving Hobart in Tasmania. I clamber out of my bunk and pull on stretch pants and a long-sleeved shirt. I notice the pools of light spilling outward from the nav station—the radar and the charting software on the laptop computer are running in addition to the chart plotter.

The minute I step into the cockpit, the scent of flowers fills my nostrils, a heady, sweet honeysuckle scent so strong that the air feels like syrup in my lungs. A light flashes out of the darkness, momentarily blinding me, then moves on. Evans hops down from his perch on the cockpit seat. "That was the lighthouse on Cape Reinga. We're about five miles offshore. There are freighters and fishing boats everywhere. You keep watch up here and I'll go down and track targets on the radar. The wind's going light, so I'll put the motor on in case we have to maneuver. Roll up the jib if it starts to luff."

In my semi-comatose state, it takes me several minutes to process this barrage of instructions. While I'm working through it, I clamber onto the cockpit seat and begin scanning the horizon. The jumble of red, green, and white lights all around us startles me awake. I try to sort through them and figure out which are connected to which and in what direction they are all moving. "Large freighter to port of us," I call down to Evans. "Looks like it's moving north."

"Three miles distant," he responds. That gives me some sense of depth in the pitch darkness of the night. The beam from the lighthouse sweeps by again, orienting me to land.

"Looks like two fishing boats trawling close to shore," I say.

"Yeah, keep an eye on them—they've come close to us once already."

For the next three hours we work our way along the twenty miles of coastline on the northern shore of the North Island, identifying each vessel and determining its speed and direction. On several occasions Evans comes into the cockpit to help me sort out a particularly confusing set of lights—one turns out to be a trawler passing down the length of an anchored freighter—and several times we alter course decisively to give right-of-way to privileged vessels. By the time we clear North Cape and turn south down the east coast of the North Island, we have encountered two dozen vessels, and Evans has been on watch for seven hours. I shoo him off to bed, set the sails, turn off the engine, and go below to make a log entry.

I'm writing a short comment about the unexpected traffic over the top of the North Island when I hear what sounds like a flock of birds squeaking and squealing from astern. It is still pitch dark—not a time for birds, unless we've plowed through a group asleep on the water's surface. Flashlight in hand, I go out on deck to be greeted by explosive pops like champagne bottles being uncorked all around the boat. I hurry forward to the bow, where I turn on the flashlight. Fifteen common dolphins swarm beneath my feet, so many they swim in two tiers in the bow wave. A quick sweep of the light and I see that we are surrounded by a pod of at least a hundred. I can hardly keep up with them with the flashlight as they dart and turn, knife out of the water and fall back, weave under the bow, then take up station in the stern wave.

I turn off the flashlight and sit down on the bow, immersed in their presence. As the first gray light of predawn seeps up from the horizon, I can make out their fins as they cut the surface of the water. As the sky turns rosy and the pink stain spreads toward us across the sea's surface, I see their shapes darting under the bow, watch as they turn on their sides to stare up at me as I stare down at them. By the time the orange ball of the sun separates itself from the horizon, I can make out every nuance of the shading on their sides, from white to fawn to olive green to gray to black, and I think I can read the curious expression in their eyes.

While I sit there, memories of the forty landfalls we have made on *Silk* and on *Hawk* wash over me. Each is indelibly etched in my mind, unique, the feeling still as fresh and real as the day it happened.

Fear and anguish tinge my memories of our very first landfall, in Bermuda, after the worst weather we've experienced in 75,000 sailing miles. All I wanted to do was find a plane to take me away from this wet, uncomfortable thing that was supposed to be my home. On our first landfall aboard *Hawk*, the south coast of Newfoundland emerged from a fogbank so suddenly and unexpectedly that it made me gasp. The last time we made landfall here, on New Zealand's North Island, we reached down this coast under a full moon, weaving our way through the off-lying islands in flat-calm waters with a 15-knot breeze on the beam. I stood on the bow in sea boots and foul-weather gear, the first time I'd worn either in two years of tropical cruising aboard *Silk*, and watched the dawn come, the light striking the drops of dew on the deck and turning them into diamonds. So many incredible memories, and the dolphins have just given me another.

Our fortieth landfall began with freighters and fishing boats. It ends when the pod leaves, all at once and as suddenly as they had come.

Smokehouse Bay, Port Fitzroy
Great Barrier Island, North Island, New Zealand

May 7, 2004

SLEEP coils away from me like smoke, and I slowly become aware of the weight of Evans's arm across my waist, the delicious warmth of his stomach against my back. I feel *Hawk* shift against her chain, hear the snubber creak against the bow roller.

The realization comes to me slowly, out of the misty dream images and half-formed thoughts of waking. Five years. We've now been cruising aboard *Hawk* for five years.

That time has slipped by so quickly, and not in the least like time goes by ashore. I can remember when weekends and vacations punctuated the cycle of my life; when I kept my watch five minutes fast in order to steal extra time at some point during the day. I can remember always being rushed, and viewing time as something never, ever to be "wasted," a commodity to be used or lost forever. The pressure and priorities of life ashore made me schedule myself down to the minute, and a traffic jam or a line at a grocery store could ruin my day by putting me behind by a quarter of an hour. I never had time to chat with the postman or to invite my neighbor in for a cup of coffee. I took a certain fierce pride in being far too busy to do nothing at all. And yet time often seemed to be moving at a snail's pace, such as during that never-ending week before a vacation or the last few hours on Friday afternoon when the hands of the clock ground to a halt.

Now I measure time in sunrises and sunsets, in winter storm seasons and tropical cyclone seasons. We need our watches to tell us the day of the week or month, not the hour. Our days move fluidly, not in fits and starts, and they disappear so quickly that we are left wondering where they have gone. Ashore I chased after time and never caught it; I was a prisoner bound by my watch and my datebook. Out here, time slips through my fingers as softly as sand. I no longer try to stop it.

Yesterday Evans and I got up with the sun and ate breakfast, then I got to work on an article about Tasmania. I was caught up in the writing, the words materializing on the computer screen almost effortlessly. I heard Tim from the catamaran stop by and give Evans some smoked fish, then I heard our outboard sputter to life and knew that Evans was going for a visit. When he came back, I had reached the end of a section. We ate the smoked fish with the bread I had baked the day before while he told me about the boat that had come in that morning, a sister ship to *Hawk* built in steel. We went ashore and found Dave and Roz—Kiwis on a 30-foot boat who have been visiting Great Barrier Island for the last twenty years—getting ready to go for a hike. They escorted us to the top of a grassy headland where Port Fitzroy lay spread out at our feet, tucked into green-clad hills. On the way, they explained to us the nuances of legislation to make the foreshore and seabed crown property and why the indigenous Maori had marched to Wellington in protest against it. By the time we got back, the sun had slipped below the rim of the hills. We ate dinner, and Evans listened to BBC radio while I worked on my journal. In bed we made love, and then sleep came quickly, our bodies and minds pleasantly exhausted.

And we have discovered that what we choose to do when we have all the time in the world says far more about us than what we have to do to make a living. Time is the price we pay to know ourselves, to find out who we really are, to grow into who we would hope to be.

A typical day, yet no day is typical. We live in a constantly shifting kaleidoscope where water, sun, wind, friends, sailing, writing, boat work, wildlife, physical exertion, and beautiful places combine endlessly to form new patterns. And we have discovered that what we choose to do when we have all the time in the world says far more about us than what we have to do to make a living. Time is the price we pay to know ourselves, to find out who we really are, to grow into who we would hope to be.

By society's standards we have given up a great deal to be out here—money, status, security. But with Evans's arms warm around me, I know we are rich beyond dreaming, blessed beyond imagining. I can only hope we might have five more years like these.

36° 37' S, 174° 48' E

Gulf Harbour Marina, Whangaparaoa
North Island, New Zealand

June 5, 2004

UNTIL then we'd been taking by the shovelful from everybody we met. It felt so good to finally be able to give something back." Tom's long ginger mustache twitches as he smiles, remembering.

Evans and I have joined Tom Harper and his wife, Christine, on their Petersen 44, *Mahurangi*, for drinks and conversation. Kiwis by birth, they lived in the United States before buying and fitting out *Mahurangi* in Seattle. Over the course of six to seven years, they cruised Mexico, then crossed the Pacific to New Zealand. We met them a few weeks ago in Gulf Harbour Marina, about thirty miles north of Auckland, where we plan to spend the winter while they return to the tropics. Tom is describing helping a young cruising couple they met in Fiji learn to navigate coral waters. "Do you know what I mean?" he finishes.

I know exactly what he means.

When Evans and I left on our first voyage aboard our Shannon 37 ketch, *Silk*, we could hardly have had less experience. We bought the boat sight unseen in January 1992 when we were living in Sweden, and shipped it to the original builder to be refit for offshore. We moved aboard in mid-May, daysailed half a dozen times around Newport, Rhode Island, then left for Bermuda in early June. Three days later we found ourselves in a force 10 storm in the Gulf Stream in waves that towered over *Silk*'s mizzenmast and cross seas that slammed into her beam like freight trains. We ran under bare poles trailing warps for forty-eight hours, and we were so seasick that neither of us could keep anything down, including water, for three days. When we finally made it to Bermuda, Neptune had defeated me in the first round.

My sailing career would have ended right there if it hadn't been for the experienced crews aboard the two dozen salt-scrubbed yachts in St. George's Harbour. Though I can't remember any of their names or the names of their boats, I can still remember the words they used. "Someday you'll realize how lucky you were to face this on your first passage. Chances are you'll never see another storm like that even if you sail all the way around the world." "In twenty years of ocean sailing, I've never been in a survival storm like the one you're describing." "You did all the right things and you and *Silk* came through just fine. You've learned more in your first six hundred miles than you'll learn in your next six thousand."

Those sailors gave Evans and me the courage to keep sailing. And every place along the way, we learned from other cruisers. In the Canaries, an experienced hand at passagemaking showed me how to store all my produce so it would last for several weeks without refrigeration in ninety-degree temperatures. In the Caribbean, West Coast sailors offered us advice for safely transiting the Panama Canal. In the Pacific, we were given charts and detailed instructions for visiting the Ha'apai group in Tonga. We, too, took by the shovelful, but we weren't giving anything back.

Like Tom, I remember when the tide turned. Walking down the dock in Hout Bay, near Cape Town in South Africa, we came upon a South African yacht that had arrived a few days earlier. The decks were festooned with foul-weather gear and cushions, and a broken boom lay on the dock. The couple aboard had rounded the Cape of Good Hope in a storm, and they were still in a state of shock. "I never imagined it could be so bad," the woman said, tears coming to her eyes. "We planned to go to the Caribbean, but now . . ."

"We had just forty knots of wind," her husband said. "But the waves . . ." he ran out of words. He swallowed and continued. "We made it through, just barely. But all the guys around here talk about sixty knots or seventy . . ."

Evans and I looked at each other. Evans said, "We had a storm like yours on our first offshore passage. It was the best thing that could have happened to us. Ever since we've been able to look around and say we've seen worse." We told them how rare 40 knots of wind was, how terrifying it was the first time, how difficult these waters were, how much more predictable and moderate tropical weather would be.

I don't know whether or not that couple quit. But in that moment, on that dock, Evans and I made a first payment on the debt we owed to countless other sailors who had helped us along the way. And for the very first time, we felt like full-fledged members of the cruising community.

Whangarei
North Island, New Zealand

July 15, 2004

Living the life we live, we encounter the most extraordinary people, and sometimes get to know them well enough to call them friends. We see evidence of their past in the fine spiderweb of lines around eyes that have spent a lifetime squinting at far horizons; in the broad-based, rolling walk that has kept them safely on deck in force 10 gales; and in the calm, matter-of-fact approach that has helped them overcome seemingly insurmountable odds. One of the most unforgettable sailor/adventurers we have ever met isn't even a person but a cat—a cat named Halifax.

Anyone who has read Alvah Simon's book *North to the Night* will remember Halifax. The tortoiseshell kitten adopted Alvah and Diana in Halifax, Nova Scotia, in 1994 when they were on their way north to spend the winter in the Arctic ice aboard their 36-foot cutter, *Roger Henry*. Within a day of freezing the boat into the ice near Bylot Island, well above the Arctic Circle in northern Canada, Diana learned that her father had been diagnosed with terminal lung cancer. In case you haven't read the book, I won't tell you how she managed it, but she did get to be with her father in his last moments, and Alvah ended up in the perpetual dark and soul-shriveling cold of the Arctic winter—alone except for Halifax, their flea-market giveaway.

To this day, Alvah credits Halifax with helping to keep him alive through that long, dark winter. The cat features in many stories in the book, and we've been fortunate to hear even more from Alvah and Diana. Of all of these, my favorite was when Alvah and Diana went out for a walk in the Arctic spring and found themselves following along in Halifax's tracks. The cat had gone out earlier, and Alvah and Diana sauntered along her trail, enjoying the warm sunshine and the signs of the changing season. After they'd been walking about ten minutes, they noticed Arctic fox tracks mixed in with Halifax's. They quickened their pace when they realized that the fox was stalking the cat, no doubt eager for a warm meal after the lean Arctic winter.

Alvah and Diana were almost running when they reached the top of a small hill and looked down the other side. Halifax was sitting in the middle of a snowfield in a sheltered bowl surrounded by low hills. As they started over the crest of the hill, they caught sight of the white Arctic fox just as it launched itself at the tortoiseshell cat. Halifax deftly clipped it across the side of the head with one large paw, sending the fox off yelping with its tail between its legs.

When we met Alvah and Diana in 1997, Alvah was working on his book, Diana was enjoying gardening, and Halifax was terrorizing the dogs around the Maine house where they were temporarily living. At the end of 2001, Alvah and Diana arrived here in New Zealand aboard the *Roger Henry* and bought a *bach*, the Kiwi term for a summer cottage, near Whangarei, on the North Island. While Alvah still dreamed of exotic landfalls, his two ladies were ready for a home that didn't need to be anchored, a garden with songbirds, and some warm sunshine.

Ever since we reached New Zealand a few months ago, we have been eager to see our friends. But first Alvah was away delivering a boat from Australia to New Zealand, then we were busy getting *Hawk* settled in to her winter berth and starting our winter refit, and after that Evans crewed a sailboat up to

Fiji with some friends. Now our schedules have finally meshed, and we have driven up to Whangarei in the car we purchased for our year in New Zealand.

We find Alvah and Diana living in a lovely open-plan wooden bungalow with views of the Pacific beyond rugged, hobbit-like peaks. Alongside the gate leading through the wooden fence and into Diana's garden hangs a ship's bell next to a sign that reads, "Home is the sailor." Halifax is ten years old now, a large-boned tortoiseshell cat with a white bib that goes right up over her nose. Her ears have white tips where they got frostbitten in the Arctic, and she moves with a studied purposefulness that gives her an air of great dignity. She's not affectionate, but wise and thoughtful, a cat that has seen and done things that no ordinary cat ever dreamed of.

Despite the idyllic nature of their existence, Alvah is working on the *Roger Henry* and talking about the Kamchatka peninsula, in Siberia. Diana has grown tired of her garden and become interested in the weaving done on the remote islands of Japan. And Halifax seems restless at times, sitting on the porch and lifting her nose to the cold Antarctic breeze blowing up from the south.

Even when they finally find it, some sailors just can't manage to stay at home.

36° 46′ S, 174° 50′ E

Hauraki Gulf, off Auckland
North Island, New Zealand

August 22, 2004

For the first time in three months, *Hawk* races the wind, free and untethered, her movements no longer checked by the spiderweb of docklines that have held her captive through the Southern Hemisphere winter. Over her bow, the slender column of the Sky Tower dominates Auckland's skyline some six miles to the south of us, every detail visible in air washed clean by the passage of a violent winter low. Our friend Steph concentrates as she drives the boat while her year-old son, Silas, plays in the cockpit at my feet. Evans stands by the backstay, keeping an eye on a cloud to the west that might herald a fast-moving squall.

"So, was it worth coming all this way?" I ask Steph. She answers with a wide smile.

We first met Steph and her husband, Chris, last winter in Fremantle, Australia. They had just returned from a year's sailing adventure aboard a Vancouver 27. In their mid-thirties, Steph very pregnant with Silas, and trying to deal with being land-based once again, they walked the docks at the Fremantle Sailing Club like a pair of ghosts yearning for a world they could no longer inhabit. They were particularly taken with *Hawk* because they dreamed of building an aluminum boat and setting sail again within the next five years, taking a child or two along. Though we were in Fremantle for almost seven months, boat repairs and Steph's difficult cesarean delivery kept us from taking them sailing. But we continued to correspond and were impressed when their enthusiasm remained undiminished by the realities of their first child.

When Steph sent us an e-mail a few months ago in which she worried over double-handing a boat *Hawk*'s size, we suggested they come spend some time aboard. Chris couldn't get away from work, so Steph committed to six hours of flying time each way—alone with a baby that had just turned one. She would have only four days when we might get out for a sail, and we all hoped that the late-winter weather would cooperate.

Things hadn't looked promising the previous week. An intense winter storm parked itself off the east coast of New Zealand, and day after day when we turned on the local weather radio, the weather buoys in the Hauraki Gulf were reporting 40-knot winds with gusts to 50. Even so, Steph's impending arrival motivated us to get the boat back into sailing shape. Evans reinstalled our reanodized portlights in the pouring rain, and our sailmaker delivered our sails to us while *Hawk* jigged against her lines in the 30-knot gusts that found their way into the marina. Two days before Steph and Silas were due to arrive, the low finally moved off, and the wind with it. By the time I picked them up at the airport, *Hawk* was ready to leave the dock—and so were we.

Hawk carries an extra reef in her sail so as not to scare the baby, and one of us keeps our attention and a steadying hand dedicated to him. But Silas has taken everything in stride, cooing with pleasure at the water racing by *Hawk*'s side and laughing up at me from among the makeshift toys littered around the playpen of *Hawk*'s cockpit. He doesn't mind a stranger taking charge of him, or the fact that his mother routinely disappears to try out the sail handling for herself.

Steph has told us how many of their friends considered her crazy for being willing to fly so far alone with the baby just to sail a boat. As Silas stands clinging to my knee and playing with a winch handle, I remember how hard it had been for Evans and me to keep our sailing dream alive through four years ashore while we were building *Hawk*. It would have been so much more difficult with children, would have taken so much more determination. If anyone can do it, I think Steph and Chris can. But whether or not they go cruising again, their dream will make Silas a much more adventurous and interesting person.

New beginnings. We're starting another sailing season, looking forward to more adventures in exotic places. Chris and Steph are dreaming of a new beginning afloat. And Silas? One of a new generation of sailors, starting young.

As the boat heels to a gust, I put my hand on Silas's stomach to steady him. He leans into my palm, spreads his arms like wings, and laughs with pure delight.

35° 01' S, 173° 46' E

Waitapu Bay, Whangaroa
North Island, New Zealand

December 25, 2004

AND in other news, the Sydney-to-Hobart Race committee has just announced that a major storm with forty-five-knot sustained southwest winds and seas in excess of seven meters is expected to hit the fleet late Monday . . ."

"Uh-oh," I say. Evans stops unwrapping his present and reaches over the wreckage of Christmas paper and ribbons to turn on the chart plotter. When the map of New Zealand comes up, Evans punches the keys until he can see the whole Tasman Sea.

"Twelve hundred miles from us," he says, calculating quickly. "That means it could be here as early as Wednesday afternoon." He doesn't have to say anything more.

Evans and I have been sitting in Whangaroa Harbour, at the top of the North Island of New Zealand, for the last three weeks. We're waiting for a weather window to make the 490-mile run down the island's west coast to Nelson, at the top of the South Island. Though six hundred to a thousand foreign yachts clear into New Zealand every year, only a handful of these ever ventures south of Auckland, less than halfway down the North Island. We are no exception. Over the course of two extended stays aboard two different boats, we have spent more than a year within 200 miles of where we cleared in. Our plan this spring is to sail to the South Island as early as possible so we'll have all summer to enjoy its wilderness of mountains, glaciers, and fjords.

It had seemed counterintuitive to make our way to the South Island, and then to Fiordland, on the island's southwest corner, by sailing down the exposed west coast—battered by the Southern Ocean swell and with almost no safe refuges—rather than daysailing in the island's lee down the east coast, with its many well-protected harbors. Yet that was the unanimous advice from Kiwi friends who have circumnavigated both islands. They assured us that the west coast route is shorter and easier than sailing down the sheltered east coast and then bucking the strong winds and currents in Cook Straits, between the two islands, or in Foveaux Strait, at the bottom of the South Island. "Just wait for a summer high-pressure system to come through," they told us. "The northeast winds will get you down the coast in no time."

So we left our winter berth near Auckland in late November and made our way over the course of several weeks to this harbor, near the top of the North Island, to wait for a high-pressure system. But summer has been slow in coming, and day after day the weather report has called for southwest gales and 12- to 15-foot swells along New Zealand's west coast. As we entered our third week in Whangaroa waiting for that elusive high, we were beginning to seriously doubt our friends' advice. But last night, on Christmas Eve, we got a forecast for three days of northerly winds starting Monday, the day after Christmas— just long enough for us to make the run to Nelson. We agreed to relax and enjoy our Christmas, then head out at first light on Monday morning, planning to arrive in Nelson on Thursday. But this chance-heard news item at the top of the hour on ABC (Australian Broadcasting Corporation) radio just shortened our three-day window by a critical twenty-four hours.

The child in me wants to ignore what we've just heard, but the sailor in me can't. "If I start stowing now, we can be underway in two hours."

Evans searches my face. "I wasn't going to ask you to give up our Christmas."

"This weather window *is* our Christmas," I answer.

The passage proves uneventful except for ABC radio's reports of the havoc wreaked by the storm on the Sydney-to-Hobart fleet. Almost half the boats retire, and the two largest maxi racers are abandoned after each incurs structural damage. Those limping into Hobart report 50-knot winds and 9-meter seas. As that same storm bears down upon us, we feel its oppressive presence lurking just over the horizon, and we push *Hawk* harder than we normally would. Leaving a day early means the northeast wind has not yet filled in, so we find ourselves sailing into a dying southerly breeze and a large swell for the first twelve hours. After that we have mostly light winds from just about every direction. We pass New Plymouth, our only option for seeking shelter, just as we receive the first storm warning in the 24-hour prognosis for our sea area.

If we hadn't heard that news item on Christmas Day, we would have received this forecast halfway down this coast and found ourselves on a lee shore with nowhere to run. Instead, with 150 miles to go, we strike out across the wide mouth of Cook Straits. Exactly three days after we left Whangaroa, at midday on Wednesday, we motor into the marina in Nelson.

Less than twelve hours later, the wind howling in the rigging wakes me from a deep sleep, reminding me of what a difference a day can make.

45° 48' S, 166° 37' E

Dusky Sound, Fiordland
South Island, New Zealand

January 23, 2005

A WASH of pink from the setting sun suffuses the sky, gentling the rugged landscape and turning the high-mountain peaks over *Hawk*'s bow into soft silhouettes that melt one into the other. I stand on the stern luxuriating in the last of the day's warmth and listening to the flutelike calling of the bellbirds and the soft murmur of the fast-flowing, peat-stained stream a hundred feet behind me. The view accords perfectly with the name Captain Cook gave this fjord on first sighting it in 1770— "duskey Bay," now Dusky Sound.

Dusky is one of thirteen narrow fjords carved into New Zealand's southwest coast by glaciers spilling down from the ice cap that covered the southern Alps during the last ice age. The fjords are known for two things besides their remoteness and natural beauty: rain and sand flies.

The high mountains that back the fjords block the progress of low-pressure systems cruising through the Southern Ocean, resulting in vast quantities of rain—25 feet or more per year. The rain qualifies as a deluge much of the time, thundering on the coach roof hour after hour. The glacier-scoured rock ridges that line the fjords cannot absorb the water but are instead transformed by it.

Two weeks ago, when the rain eased from a downpour to a drizzle for the first time in a week, we sailed to the head of Doubtful Sound, about fifty miles to the north. As the light breeze nudged *Hawk* down the fjord, the sunlight spilled from the clouds in long fingers that brushed across the pewter sea, burnishing it silver. The 3,000- to 5,000-foot-high mountains lining the channel receded into the distance shimmering like a mirage. Cascades of water plunged down sheer faces of scoured gray rock and irregular seams of granite before flashing white from deep within the dense tangle of temperate rain forest. In some places these falls were little more than lacy plumes swept away by the wind; in others they were full-fledged cataracts growling in a low voice as they tumbled for hundreds of feet. At any given moment we had from three to a dozen waterfalls within sight; their delicate white tracery looked like lace worked into the green and gray faces of the rugged peaks.

The near constant runoff creates a freshwater layer some six feet deep on top of the seawater of the fjord. This provides the perfect habitat for the other thing for which the sounds are well known: sand flies, the vicious little biting insects that swarm anything warm-blooded. Our cockpit is littered with their corpses, felled by a mosquito coil that has been burning under the hard dodger. The sand flies disappear completely only during the hardest rainfall, and are usually thickest in calm weather, such as I am enjoying now. This is the first time in almost a month I have stood outside and been warm and dry and bug-free, and I fully appreciate the utter perfection of this moment.

Only two of the fjords of the thirteen in Fiordland are accessible by road. Visitors to these are herded from buses into tour boats for a fast two-hour cruise up the sound and back. They pass through the landscape, and only if they are lucky do they see anything more than the base of the mountains on either side of the channel underneath the low-lying clouds. Dusky Sound cannot be reached by road, but only by a demanding four-day hike, by floatplane, or by boat from the Southern Ocean. Those hardy enough to brave the rain and the sand flies to hike into Dusky can get only as far as the head of the fjord, so they miss the essence of the sound's beauty, the ever-changing interplay of light and cloud and water that I am now admiring.

Hawk is the magic carpet that transports us to other worlds, letting us immerse ourselves in extraordinary places that would otherwise remain far beyond our reach. By being here aboard *Hawk*, we do more than pass through. For a brief period of time we experience this landscape, become part of it. The rain drips off our noses and down the collars of our jackets; we scratch at the red welts left by sand fly bites; we feel the rumble of the waterfalls through the decks; we steady ourselves against the steep Southern Ocean swell as we sail out of each fjord.

We do not view this place through the window of a tour boat, nor do we climb on a bus at the end of the day and leave it behind. So when the sky finally clears and the setting sun kisses the heavens, making them blush, it is for us alone.

Port Pegasus, Stewart Island
Sixty miles south of South Island, New Zealand
January 26, 2005

THE bright sunlight streaming in through the hatch over our bunk wakes me. I blink at it. I can't quite figure out why sunshine should have brought me out of a sound sleep, why it seems so unusual and unfamiliar. Sunshine! I come fully awake in an instant and throw off the covers. Evans stirs sleepily. "What's up?"

"It's sunny out!" I pad across the cabin sole toward the companionway. A quick glance at the clock over the nav station shows it is just before seven in the morning. Less than five hours' sleep, and I feel renewed. After almost a month in New Zealand's Fiordland, I have grown tired of the constant drumming of rain on the coach roof, of moody gray skies, of gloomy days that creep from black to dark gray to black again.

We left Dusky Sound the morning before, planning to make landfall on Stewart Island, thirty miles beyond the bottom of the South Island, right around this time. But *Hawk* had other ideas. For the first time since we left the top of the North Island almost two months ago, we had a quartering wind and moderate seas. *Hawk* seemed eager to remind us of just how well she can sail cracked off the wind and unhampered by a twelve-foot swell. She raced along at 8 to 9 knots, even after we shortened sail. We rounded Stewart Island's Southwest Cape around midnight just as a plump orange moon broke free of the few remaining clouds along the horizon. With Southwest

Cape behind us, we had now passed under all five of the Southern Ocean capes aboard *Hawk*.

After that, the 3-knot current running under Stewart Island assisted *Hawk's* efforts, and we arrived off the entrance to Port Pegasus at a little after one in the morning, with the moon high and streaming a silver carpet out the channel to greet us. With the radar, GPS, depth sounder, and good visibility, we felt confident negotiating the entrance and working our way into a cove where we could anchor. In the bright moonlight, we were able to see where the silver gray of the water met the hard edge of the shore, and the dark silhouettes of the low hills against the brighter horizon. But that was only enough to form a vague and incomplete picture of the world that now surrounds us.

I pause at the bottom of the companionway with my hand on the hatch, anticipating the moment of discovery. A landfall made during daylight involves a slow and steady familiarization, a refining of details as the land comes gradually into focus, then grows from miniature to human scale. But with night landfalls, we arrive to a shadow world and in the morning get to enter it whole, erupting upward out of *Hawk's* belly, born again. I close my eyes, throw back the hatch, and step into the cockpit before I let myself look.

Hawk lies in a horseshoe cove surrounded by low hills covered with a mixture of knee-high scrub and skeletal trees. Great mounds of rock jut up at odd intervals, some rising to smooth domes of granite a thousand feet high or more. Not a breath of wind stirs the water's surface, and the shoreline, the scrub, the hills, the granite domes, and *Hawk* herself hover over their mirror images. I catch my breath at the beauty of the scene just as Evans comes on deck. "Look," he says. He points to the water, and beneath the reflections I see a fur seal spiraling toward us. It surfaces just off our bow—marring the mirrored scenery with small ripples—and stares, inspecting us with large, liquid eyes.

It dives again and somersaults under the boat, plainly visible below the perfect reflections above it, a moving image super-imposed upon the still one.

I am so mesmerized that I jump when something leaps out of the water a hundred feet in front of us. It erupts from the water again, and this time I see a stout black and white torpedo with pink feet and yellow on its head. It porpoises up until its whole body is visible, then arcs back down, only to rocket up again. It takes me a full minute to realize that it is a yellow-eyed penguin, the rarest of all the penguin species, moving faster than any penguin I have ever seen.

I take Evans's hand, and he smiles at me. A whole new day, in a brand-new world.

45° 52′ S, 170° 34′ E

Otago Yacht Club, Dunedin
South Island, New Zealand

March 14, 2005

I STAND in the companionway and survey the confusion of cardboard boxes and canvas bags covering every flat surface in the cockpit and every square inch of the cabin sole below me. Packages of flour, sugar, rice, and pasta spill out of bags onto the cockpit seats; cases of shelf-stable milk and juice lie scattered across the cabin sole; a dozen bottles of spices, a half dozen toothbrushes, jars of hot chocolate mix, and super-saver-size packages of batteries drift across the tabletop in the main saloon.

I left the boat at seven this morning for the two-mile walk into the New World grocery store, at the center of Dunedin. It has taken me all day to get this far—to stack three carts with everything on my six-page list, to go through the checkout line and get $800 worth of groceries bagged and boxed, to stuff it all into a taxi on the street in front of the store, then to pile it on the lawn of the Otago Yacht Club before enlisting Evans's aid in humping it out the dock and across the boat to which we're rafted. Now everything is aboard, but the sun is getting low and I'm worn out. It will take me another day to securely stow our next three to four months of provisions.

I sense the tension in him, a familiar aspect of the days before a departure. He likes to say that every successful cruising couple consists of an optimist and a pessimist. The optimist gets them off the dock; the pessimist keeps them from losing the boat.

We arrived in Dunedin, on the southeast corner of New Zealand's South Island, three weeks ago after an exhilarating fifteen-hour sail from Stewart Island averaging 10 knots over the ground running before 40 knots of wind. Since then we have been enjoying the hospitality of the Otago Yacht Club and exploring the university town of 100,000 christened by home-sick Scottish settlers with the Celtic name for Edinburgh. But now the summer is drawing to a close, and our time in New Zealand with it. In the next few days we will leave on the first of three 2,700-mile passages that will scribe a sloppy S across the face of the mighty Pacific and take us from New Zealand to French Polynesia to Hawaii to British Columbia.

While I've been provisioning, Evans has been hard at work with his own preparations. The staysail and trysail have been hanked on and bagged. The jacklines have been secured to cleats at either end of the boat. He has deflated the dinghy and stowed it below along with our solar panel. Our storm jibs lie on the sole of the head near the companionway; our drogues have been lashed to the heater in the main cabin. As I watch, he removes the chain from the shank of the anchor and attaches it to the plug for our hawsehole before sealing the plug in place with silicone. When he finishes, he returns to the cockpit wiping silicone from his hands.

I sense the tension in him, a familiar aspect of the days before a departure. He likes to say that every successful cruising couple consists of an optimist and a pessimist. The optimist gets them off the dock; the pessimist keeps them from losing the boat. Right now he is the pessimist, going over every aspect of the hull and rig in his mind, searching out any weakness.

But as I look at *Hawk*'s clean decks and feel her tug against the docklines, a surge of anticipation tingles through me. It has been a full year since we have made an offshore passage, and two full years since we have made a passage of more than 2,000 miles. And I have missed it. Many cruisers view passages as a necessary evil to get them from one place to another, but for me passages have always been a way to cleanse myself, to let go of the unceasing busyness of shore life and come to a quiet place inside myself that I cannot seem to reach any other way. The sea lays me bare and humbles me; then it scrubs me clean and makes me whole again. In the process it replenishes the wellspring of my creativity, nourishing the writer in me just as much as the sailor.

All of these rituals—from the provisioning, which has engaged me all day, to the mast inspection, which took us most of yesterday afternoon—are steps in a familiar dance that lead from the safety of shore to the uncertainty of the sea. These steps comfort and reassure us. They prepare us mentally as much as physically. They turn trepidation into anticipation, caution into confidence. They make it possible for us to untie the docklines and step off into the unknown.

Dunedin, New Zealand to Raivavae, Austral Islands
13th day of passage

April 2, 2005

As I reach the top step of the companionway, *Hawk* rears up until all I can see is her bow silhouetted against the bruised gray of the sky. I brace myself as the bow starts to drop, but she settles gently, leaving churning patches of bright blue water covered with a lacework of white in her wake. Before her bow rises again, I look out over the restless expanse of heaving water, where the gusts whip the tumbling white crests into spume and spit them in streaks across the face of the blue-black seas. *Hawk* feels besieged and embattled, clinging to her course despite the opposition of a hostile sea.

This is the third and worst front that has slammed into us in the two weeks since we left Dunedin, at the bottom of New Zealand, bound for French Polynesia. Each successive front has brought stronger winds out of the northeast, right up our course. We have now been forereaching under the double-reefed mainsail for more than twenty-four hours, and the winds—instead of moderating as predicted—have steadily increased, and the seas with them. The anemometer now dances around 40 knots, with an occasional jump up to 45. Although the waves are not the worst we have seen, they have gotten big enough that I have lost any frame of reference that would allow me to estimate their size.

I hand Evans one of the granola bars I have brought up from below. We eat without tasting, out of necessity for the energy condensed in the oats and dried fruit rather than from desire.

The boat rears up for the next wave, but this time she pauses as if surprised not to find anything on the other side. She lurches out from under me as her bow crashes down into the trough with a jarring thud that resonates from the soles of my feet to the top of my skull. Evans swears softly.

A hissing sound causes me to brace myself as a wave comes roaring in at a 60-degree angle to the others, its top a churning mass of foam. It catches *Hawk* just aft of the mast with a solid "thwunk," sending her staggering sideways, then washes down the decks and straight over the top of the hard dodger to fall in a thundering curtain of whitewater into the cockpit just behind where Evans sits. When *Hawk* snaps back upright, only my white-knuckled grip on the handhold just inside the companionway keeps me from getting tossed down below.

We are completely and totally isolated, disconnected, floating free in space and time. No one else knows what is happening here aboard *Hawk*. Even I, surrounded by the wind-whipped water, cannot grasp the scene around me in its entirety. It comes to me in a series of sharp-focused details from freeze-framed snapshots. Frothing fingers of whitewater thick as cotton curling over a wave's dark face. A distorted view of the bow through a sheet of seawater thrown across the hard dodger. The textured stubble of tan and gray thrown across the delicate shadows in Evans's gaunt cheeks.

Time stretches, then ceases to exist. Past and future fall away. The incessant monologue inside my head stutters to a halt. I live only in the clash of wills between *Hawk* and each rumbling wave. In the instant in which I exist, these things—the boat's restless movements, the delicate tracery of spume on the blue-black sea, the rumbling bass note of the wind, Evans's comforting presence—engulf me and overwhelm me, stripping me to my essence.

Nothing else matters.

THIRTY-six hours later, the rich, yeasty smell of fresh-baked bread wafts up to me where I stand at the top of the companionway, inundating my senses until I can almost taste the golden loaves cooling on the stove top. *Hawk*'s long, rolling motion as she surges from wave to wave rocks me gently, soothing the tight knots from my shoulders and back. The stiff trade-wind breeze filling her twin headsails dances with the clothes hung out to dry on the lifelines, then rushes headlong into the cabin below and out the open hatches and ports. The wind's cool breath caresses my shockingly white arms and legs, bare for the first time in many months. *Hawk* feels light and free, totally unencumbered, the sea her ally as we fly northward over the indigo water, leaving a frothing white wake behind us.

I too feel light and free, totally unencumbered. The boundaries that define me ashore have become blurred, irrelevant. I can almost feel the intricate web of connection that binds me to each trade-wind cloud. Each breath I take links past to future. I exist in the smell of the bread and the brilliant blue of the water and the soft caress of the wind. Somehow all these have become part of me, or I have become part of them.

I smile at Evans, sitting in the shade of the hard dodger, reading a book. He senses my gaze and looks up, meeting my eyes, then gives me a slow, lazy smile in return. In the sensuous fullness of this moment, these things—the bright blue sea, *Hawk*'s rhythmic motions, the rich sensations that fill me to overflowing, the warm awareness of Evans nearby—complete me, center me, and make me whole.

All of these matter.

Honolulu, Hawaii to Prince Rupert, British Columbia
17th day of passage

June 27, 2005

LANDFALL . . . Our Pacific voyage is coming to a close. Since leaving Dunedin, at the bottom of New Zealand, at the end of March, we have spent fifty-seven days at sea and sailed more than 8,500 nautical miles. Now, for the first time since leaving Hawaii seventeen days ago, our world consists of more than just sea and sky.

With the first sight of land comes the full realization that we have reached a completely different place. Off *Hawk*'s port beam, the soft gray outlines of the mountains of southern Alaska lie etched against the azure sky. Over her bow, the rounded blue-gray hills along the northernmost coast of British Columbia rise to higher snow-speckled peaks farther inland. Nothing could be more different than the dry red and brown volcanic peaks thrusting out of the wave-tossed seas that we left in our wake more than two weeks ago. Then the nights were twelve hours long and pitch dark; last night, the first blush of dawn colored the northeastern sky before the last streaks of sunset had faded in the northwest.

Evans and I stand on the cockpit seats, leaning against the top of the hard dodger, our breath steaming in the brisk morning air as *Hawk* runs before 30 knots of wind under the reefed main and the poled-out jib. Neither of us speaks. A pleasant mixture of emotions swirls through me—satisfaction at the completion of this leg of our voyage, pride in *Hawk*'s seamanlike condition, pleasure at the beauty of this intricate coast, deep affection for Evans, and an abiding contentment with my life. The voyage has renewed me by refilling the wellspring at my creative center even as it emptied me of the need for anything beyond the sweet intoxication of each indrawn breath. I would be content to live this moment for eternity.

It will take us all day to thread our way through the channels and islands along the British Columbian coast to reach Prince Rupert. In that time, we will make the slow transition from sea to shore. I will strip the sea berths and gather the laundry, make a grocery list, and put all the books for trading into a canvas bag. I will inhale the scent of fresh-laundered sheets as I make our double berth in the forepeak and anticipate sharing it with Evans tonight. Evans will remove the trysail from its track, bag the staysail, coil and store its sheets, and remove the jacklines. He will reattach the chain to the anchor and pull the chain out on deck before flaking it back in the locker, to ensure it will run free. We will take turns keeping watch for the freighters, cruise ships, and trawlers that suddenly populate our world, and dodging the floating logs visible only because of the six seagulls standing atop each one.

By the time I let go of the anchor, we will have already begun to distance ourselves from the rhythms we have lived by for fifty-seven of the last ninety days: the heave of the sea, the rise and fall of the wind, the sun's journey across the sky, the waxing and waning of the moon, the endless rotation of the stars, and the seemingly random swirl of weather patterns. The very act of preparation will take us one step away from nature and from this Zen state of pure being. I have never been able to take ashore with me this immersion in the now. But after a passage I return renewed, awake to wonder, full of joy, and reassured that the sea awaits when I need to find myself again.

The sea transports us, but it also transforms us. It represents a doorway to the world—and to our innermost selves—open to anyone with the courage and the determination to walk through. The moment of walking through that door, of casting off the docklines, is one that will stay with you forever.

Six years ago, we spent our last night before beginning this voyage in our favorite anchorage in the Chesapeake. This tiny, tree-lined cove lay a few miles from the boatyard where we had been berthed for the last year, installing *Hawk's* interior. The following morning we pulled up our anchor, and *Hawk* hovered over her perfect reflection, unmoored, flying free over the surface of the Earth. After being nothing more than a promise for four long years, *Hawk* was instantaneously transformed into a magic carpet that could take us anywhere on the face of the globe connected by a least depth of seven feet of water to that cove on the edge of the North American continent. The constraints of time, of transportation, of logistics, of money that had become an accepted part of our lives suddenly fell away, and the endless possibilities of ocean travel took their place. In that moment, *Hawk* represented pure potential, limited only by our skills and courage.

And that, for me, sums up the voyaging life. It is a life of limitless possibilities, endless opportunities, and continuous renewal. The sea tests us constantly, demanding we learn new skills and don't get complacent about old ones. The communities we visit—and sometimes become part of—challenge our most basic assumptions about ourselves and our values, and force us to shed prejudices we didn't even know we had. The rugged, remote areas we have been privileged to spend time in and the fast-disappearing creatures that find a way to survive in the harshest conditions imaginable bring home to us the wondrous diversity—and fragility—of our planet. The other sailors we meet humble us. Some have overcome great odds to be out here; others quietly and competently complete epic voyages without fanfare or recognition.

If there is one thing that our years aboard *Hawk* and *Silk* have taught us, it is that ordinary, everyday people do the most extraordinary, inspirational things. If you've dreamed of casting off the docklines and sailing for far horizons, don't let your chance slip away. We'll be out here, where the sea meets the sky, waiting for you.

PHOTOS

Title Page, Dusky Sound, South Island, New Zealand.

Page 28, *Hawk* anchored off Barbuda.

Page 82, Doubtful Sound, South Island, New Zealand.

Page 91, Staten Island, 60 miles north of Cape Horn (Photo by Evans Starzinger).

Page 98, Commerson's dolphin off Argentina.

Page 112, Wandering albatross over Southern Ocean.

Page 134, Southern Ocean.

Page 172, Humpback whales near Puerto Eden, Chile.